STRESS
LESS
LIVING

STRESS LESS LIVING

God-Centered Solutions When
You're Stretched Too Thin

TRACIE MILES

LEAFWOOD
PUBLISHERS

an imprint of Abilene Christian University Press

STRESS-LESS LIVING

God-Centered Solutions When You're Stretched Too Thin

an imprint *of Abilene Christian University Press*

Copyright 2021 by Tracie Miles

ISBN 978-1-68426-002-7 | LCCN 2021014953

1st edition published in 2012

Printed in the United States of America

LIBRARY OF CONGRESS CATALOGING-IN-PUBLICATION DATA

Names: Miles, Tracie, 1967- author.

Title: Stress-less living : God-centered solutions when you're stretched too thin / Tracie Miles.

Description: Revised edition. | Abilene, Tex. : Leafwood Publishers, 2021. | Includes bibliographical references.

Identifiers: LCCN 2021014953 (print) | LCCN 2021014954 (ebook) | ISBN 9781684260027 (trade paperback) | ISBN 9781684269044 (ebook)

Subjects: LCSH: Christian women—Religious life. | Stress management—Religious aspects—Christianity. | Stress management for women. | Anxiety—Religious aspects—Christianity.

Classification: LCC BV4527 .M4395 2021 (print) | LCC BV4527 (ebook) | DDC 248.8/43—dc23

LC record available at https://lccn.loc.gov/2021014953

LC ebook record available at https://lccn.loc.gov/2021014954

Interior text design by Sandy Armstrong | Cover design by Faceout Studio, Molly von Borstel

Leafwood Publishers is an imprint of: Abilene Christian University Press, ACU Box 29138, Abilene, Texas 79699

1-877-816-4455 | www.leafwoodpublishers.com

21 22 23 24 25 26 27 / 8 7 6 5 4 3 2 1

To my children, Morgan, Kaitlyn, and Michael,
the greatest joys of my life. I am beyond blessed.

To my mother, Barbara,
the most amazing woman I know,
who has always been my biggest cheerleader.

Contents

" . . . you are worried and upset about many things,
but only one thing is needed . . . "

—Luke 10:41b–42a NIV

Introduction

On that particular day, the news on television had me mesmerized, and not in a good way.

Wave after wave of unsettling and shocking images streamed from our nation's Capitol Building as the protestors stormed ahead, politicians from both sides hid under seats and tables, and news crews swarmed the streets like bees fleeing a shaken hive. Every minute there was a new angle and conflicting information, as local citizens were put on curfew for their own safety. My grown children began sending family group texts with questions and concerns. We all knew history was unfolding right before our eyes, and fear was growing deep in our hearts.

Having already been another personally stressful day, I wasn't surprised when I felt a tightness in my chest begin to form—a sure sign stress was threatening to squirm its way into my spirit.

This was the first time the Capitol has been breached since the British burned the building in August 1814. The COVID-19 pandemic, which we'd all been suffering through for nine months, seemed to be getting worse instead of better. Vaccines were available for the select, not the majority. Failing businesses. Political war.

With stressors already blaring through my head, my heart was primed for more anxious thoughts to join in. Friends, family, and friends of friends who were sick with the coronavirus came to mind, along with a handful of acquaintances who had lost loved ones due to it. I thought of those who worked on the front line in hospitals, endangering not only their physical health but also their emotional and mental health. I mourned the loss of not being able to see loved ones due to pandemic shutdowns and social distancing rules.

My daughter Kaitlyn had lost her job the prior year as an American Airlines flight attendant due to the airline's layoffs, and her entire life had been uprooted, forcing her to move from New York back to our home in North Carolina. My other daughter Morgan was dealing with a great deal of anxiety, trying to work remotely as a middle school teacher with overwhelming challenges and frustrations that were out of her control. My son Michael was working diligently against all odds to finish his senior year of college virtually as an architecture major and get accepted into the master's program.

My precious mother was dealing with A-fib in her heart and a few other health issues, and my sister's multiple sclerosis was at its crippling worst, especially after recently enduring three surgeries and twelve months of chemotherapy for breast cancer. My entire family was still reeling from the strife and tension of my father's passing the year before and issues regarding inheritance. On top of everything else, I was running at mock speed at work in a fast-paced and busy environment while juggling two additional part time jobs on evenings and weekends. I could go on. And on. And on. The stress of work and all that was on my plate had me stretched thin and this was one of those days when I felt I might just snap once and for all.

Making matters even worse was that I was now having to deal with all the chaos, busyness, and stressors of life all by myself, due to my husband of twenty-five years abandoning our marriage and family five years prior, leaving me a single mom to three children and a sole provider with no full-time job, a million problems to handle, and a financial pit that was nearly impossible to climb out of. In fact, still this very week as I write these words, I was brought to tears again due to being blindsided by yet another upsetting issue in the seemingly never-ending trail of financial damage left in the aftermath of my husband's departure. These issues always tend to suck me back into the feelings of heartache, devastation, and anger over my divorce, as if it happened yesterday rather than more than five years ago.

Suddenly I felt sullen and my heart began to ache, prompting my mind to drift to places it didn't need to go. The paralyzing fear consuming every heart in the nation over sickness, politics, freedoms, and the future. Quarantines and mask mandates. Normal life and all the things we once enjoyed feeling like a thing of the past and wondering if we would ever get those freedoms and joys back. The health of my elderly loved ones. The silence of my empty nest. The status of my finances. The unknowns of my future and if I'd ever be able to retire. Should I sell my home or stay? Will I be alone when I'm older? What if this, and what if that . . . and then there is this problem, and that issue. . . . Can you relate? I have no doubt you have an entire list of your own stressors that could quickly roll off your tongue.

Sitting alone on the couch in my den, laptop resting on my knees, mind racing with all the stressful thoughts that had sprouted life from the fertilization of the disturbing news blaring all day, I felt anxiety and stress threatening to engulf me, as had happened so many times before. But this time, I chose to respond differently to the situation at hand. The stressors in my life over the past few years had been close to unbearable, and the last thing I needed was for my emotions to kick into overdrive again. I became acutely aware of what was happening. I paused. I sat up straight, shifted my thoughts, turned off the TV, and took a deep breath. I knew I had a choice to make.

I could either let the stress of my world burn a hole in my soul, opening up a gap for anxiety, anger, and panic to seep in and steal my peace and joy, or I could recognize what was happening and take the reins of my thoughts and emotions rather than letting them run wild. I knew I needed to refocus on the peace Jesus offers if we remember to turn our attention back to him and off of the craziness and chaos around us.

You see, years ago, when I was a young mom, in a different difficult season when stress was rampant in my life and I accused everything and everyone of being the cause, God opened my eyes to realize there is never a "season" of stress we have to endure. Life itself is a season, and life will always be full of trials and stress. It always has been and always be, from biblical times to the present. Yet if we truly desire to have peace in our lives and learn how to avoid letting the chaos of the world and worry over our circumstances pull us into a pit of anxiety time and time again, all we really have to do is practice habitually seeking peace in the only place it can be truly found.

I've read that the number of times the word "peace" appears in the Bible varies from one version to another, but generally it ranges from 263 to 428 instances. But this gift of peace, which is our only rescue from a life of stress, can really be summed up in one verse: "I have told you all this so that you may have peace in me. Here on earth you will have many trials and sorrows. But take heart, because I have overcome the world" (John 16:33).

Many people are under the impression the Bible is not really a resource for handling stress, much less for finding stress manage-ment tips, simply because the word "stress" is not a biblical term. Although the word "stress" was not commonly used in biblical times, Jesus referred to this disease consistently through synonyms that can be found in every Bible translation and on practically every page. Synonyms such as "anxiety," "worry," "troubles," "fears," "burdens," "anguish," "dismay," "strain," "trials," "tribulations," and "adversity," just to name a few.

He spoke of the heartache of anxieties, fears, frustrations, and betrayal, the sadness of deceit, the pull of temptation, and the devastation of sin. He tells of difficult circumstances taking place in politics, churches, relationships, marriages, families, parenting, sexual sin, and communities and the world as a whole.

Despite the differences between biblical times and the twenty-first century, the presence of stress and our need for Jesus is the same. The lack of the term "stress" certainly did not keep Jesus from understanding a stressful life or from promising the peace we would need to hear and apply in today's busy, chaotic, stressful world. It didn't keep him from voicing encouragement and reminding us of the hope that is available in him and that is applicable no matter what century we live in. Jesus knew we would be stressed, so he not only addressed it, he provided the solutions for dealing with it.

Jesus teaches us how to celebrate life, despite life. How to find joy, despite circumstances. How to overcome stress, despite the constant balancing act that we all experience. How to not only survive the storms but stay afloat in the midst of them. From Genesis to Revelation, we can discover infinite suggestions for biblical stress relief if we only seek them out. Relief that can fill us back up when we feel depleted and stretched too thin.

Although we are living in extremely stressful times, stress is not a sign of the times—it's a sign of life. Our stressors may be different today than when Jesus walked the earth, but the overwhelming sickness of stress is exactly the same. Pandemics, cancer, and other viruses or illness are not the only things we need to fear. The disease of stress is a silent killer.

Maybe you have tried every stress relief tactic known to mankind, to no avail. If so, I pray you will soon discover that all the stress management tactics in the world cannot hold a candle to the real and permanent stress relief that Jesus offers. His methods have withstood the test of time, used by generation after generation, and he is the only tried, true, and proven stress relief method there has ever been.

If you have been searching for a peace and serenity that seems completely out of reach, maybe you have simply been searching in all the wrong places.

Throughout the pages of this book, you will learn how to recognize the signs of burnout, the symptoms of chronic stress, and the potentially dire consequences of ignored stress. By pulling out stress relief secrets tucked in the Bible and God-centered solutions to managing your stress, you can soak in down-to-earth encouragement and biblical practices to help you better manage stress from your everyday life experiences, such as work, home, marriage, parenting, addictions, health, pandemics, finances, and the economy. It will also help you discover how to better deal with all the worry and anxiety life ushers in and help you embark on a new journey of living life with unshakable joy and abundant peace. This may be something you feel is impossible right now, but it actually can be your reality if you're ready and willing to put in the time and investment to change. Your circumstances may not change, but the way you handle them and deal with them can. Through faith, all things are possible. Including having peace in the midst of a chaotic life and preventing yourself from being stretched to the breaking point.

Friend, you have not picked up this book by mistake. You deserve so much more than to live a life marred by anxiety, worry, and stress. You deserve peace. You deserve happiness. And it can all be yours if you're ready to accept the challenge to live a less stressed life. If you have been longing for a fresh start, a renewed spirit, better health, and increased energy, and have a desire to live the stressed-less and abundant, joy-filled life Christ intended for you, I invite you to join me on this journey.

Give it a shot. You have nothing to lose and life to gain.

CHAPTER ONE

Discovering the Real Problem

I used to think my stress was everybody else's fault. For example, if only my boss were nicer to me, I wouldn't be so stressed out. If my salary was higher, I wouldn't be so stressed about money. If my deadlines were not so unreasonable, I wouldn't be stressed. In fact, if I didn't have to work, I wouldn't be stressed at all!

Or maybe you can relate to thoughts like this: If my husband would help me out around the house or with the kids more, I wouldn't be so stressed. If he would love me more or care more about my feelings, I wouldn't be stressed . . . If I weren't divorced. If my children would stop arguing. If parenting wasn't so exhausting. If I did not have this health issue. If my loved one wasn't sick. If my loved one hadn't passed away. If I didn't have so much debt. If my house didn't need repairs. If I could buy a new home. If my credit were better. If I could land a new job. If I had gotten that promotion I deserved. If the economy hadn't crashed. If the pandemic hadn't occurred. If my business hadn't failed. If terrorism didn't exist. If my friend hadn't betrayed me. If that person had not treated me so rudely or unfairly. If, if, if . . .

Although I have not recited all of these "if's," over the past number of years, a large majority of them have escaped my lips at one time or another. These are just a tiny sampling of the common issues people face every day that cause overwhelming stress. As we continue to carry out this ritual of reciting our "ifs," we all eventually convince ourselves that people and circumstances are the sole cause for our stressed-out lives. I spent way too many years stuck in the habit of doing just that. However, several years ago, my eyes were opened to the fact that I was trudging through my overly busy life feeling stressed and distressed over big and little things all the time. I realized not only was I stressed but life itself had become a job instead of a joy.

Where was the happiness I once knew? Why did I constantly focus on what was wrong with my life rather than appreciating what was good? Why was I always counting burdens instead of blessings? Why did I allow the actions and behaviors of other people to make me feel so afflicted, angry, incompetent, or hurt? When did I become so negative and pessimistic? When and how had I morphed into such a frazzled, fatigued, frustrated, burnt-out, overworked, overloaded, overcommitted woman? Could I ever change, feel like myself again, and enjoy the gift of life, rather than take it for granted?

As these questions swirled through my mind like debris caught in the eye of a hurricane, I knew something had to change; and through God's intervention, I gradually came to understand what had to change . . . me. Once I accepted that truth, my overall life improved. I stopped wondering what was wrong with everyone else, being upset about my circumstances, the world, and all the things out of my control, and instead began pondering the hard question: "What is wrong with me?"

As strange as it may sound, throughout the years when I endured the lengthy season of extreme stress and anxiety, I was actually blessed with a wonderful life full of family, love, financial security, a good job, and countless blessings. From the outside looking in, my life may have even seemed perfect. But from the inside looking out, the weight of stress was overshadowing my outlook, gradually choking the joy out of my heart, like a tiny but fatal weed wrapping itself around a beautiful flower, slowly squeezing out the fragile life within.

In hindsight, I can clearly see I was so caught up in my stressors and problems that I was discounting all those blessings and favors from God. I was missing the opportunity to enjoy my life because I was focused on my stressors, which seemingly consumed my every waking moment. I had forgotten what it felt like for my heart to feel light and free, detached from all the twisted and dangerous fibers of stress that had become entangled in my existence. Pure contentment and peace seemed to be a distant memory, impossible to recoup.

I couldn't remember the last time I laughed heartily at a silly movie or lounged on the couch with my children—away from my laptop—or enjoyed a leisurely walk without my mind trailing off in a dozen directions, worrying about every situation or person that came to mind. I accepted that something was wrong and had to change.

Sometimes God allows us to get to the very end of our rope, barely hanging on by one little thread, before he reaches down and pulls us up with one mighty swoop. Why? Because usually when we get to that desperate point of exhaustion, knowing we have tried to manage life on our own without success, that is the time when we fervently call out to God, and he always answers.

In Matthew 5:3, from the passage known as the Beatitudes where Jesus is teaching his disciples, we are reminded of God's desire to rescue us from ourselves. *The Message* Bible translates it this way: "You're blessed when you're at the end of your rope. With less of you there is more of God and his rule." Less of me and more of God is a delicious recipe for change.

The day I found myself clinging on to that last little frazzled strand on the rope of my life, I called out to God in a prayer of desperation. As my eyes refocused away from my problems and onto the only One who could handle them, the only One who had the power to pull me out of the stress pit I had dug myself into, I saw something new for the first time. Suddenly, I was able to gain a new perspective of the strange land I had come to live in. I finally saw my life for what it was, and I was able to understand my problem clearly for the very first time.

I recognized that stress had become the norm in my life, as opposed to the occasional exception. I saw that I was not only stressed every now and then, or over certain anxiety-inducing situations, I was stressed every day, about everything, involving everyone. While I wasn't paying attention, stress had worked itself into every part of my life. After seeing my life from God's perspective, I began to long for my old normal back. Not a perfect normal but a normal that did not exist solely on life-robbing stress.

As a result of this vision, and after much prayer, God led me to a new place—a place that required me to step out in humility, swallow my pride, and admit I had allowed stress to overshadow my faith. I had gradually put God on the back burner as I hurried through my busy days, thinking I had life figured out and could handle it on my own, all the while tripping over one stressor after another. I knew I needed to take responsibility for how I felt and make a conscious and determined commitment to God, my faith, and myself, and stop blaming everyone and everything for my stress.

What Works and What Doesn't

Before God gave me this self-revelation about the real root of my issues, I was already well aware that all my former ways of trying to cope with stress and bring about change had been woefully inadequate and ineffective.

You see, I had tried just holding in all my emotions and putting on an iron mask of calmness and strength every morning, but eventually the simplest thing would tip the scale and my façade would be blown. Then I tried just the opposite—airing all my thoughts and emotions to friends, family, and coworkers, thinking that complaining, whining, or letting people know how I felt would make me feel better—but eventually they would just grow weary of hearing me rant. I tried massages, manicures, pedicures, fancy vacations, days off from work, bubble baths, hot tubs, listening to soft music, reading books, studying stress-management books, researching the art of balancing life, grown-up time-outs, yoga, and all the other common suggestions for stress relief. I tried retail therapy, and although I love the look and feel of new clothes, shoes, and accessories and enjoy looking my best, the temporary thrill of shopping did not cure my stress either. In fact, all it did was increase my debt, which, of course, merely caused more stress. I tried having a glass of wine at night after stressful days, in the hopes my nerves might be settled in doing so. But all that accomplished was falling asleep too early, having a restless night, and then waking up with a headache the next morning.

Despite all my varied attempts at using the supposed tried-and-true stress-management methods in my quest to calm my spirit, the sensation of serenity remained out of reach. So I found myself stuck in a seemingly never-ending cycle of closing out each day with cooking and cleaning and tucking my children into bed, before collapsing in bed myself with a knot in my stomach, heaviness in my chest, an emptiness in my heart, and worries in my head, knowing that tomorrow it would just start all over again. All the while, my physical health was declining, but I was completely oblivious of the cause.

The time came when I was sick and tired of feeling sick and tired all the time! I had become desperate for an answer, and since it was glaringly obvious my circumstances and the people in my life were not apt to change any time soon, I realized I needed to do whatever it would take to get control of my stress, before my stress took complete control over my life. You see, in that moment of prayer

I mentioned earlier, I finally acknowledged that I was worried and upset about all too many things, just like Martha in Luke 10.

I never sat at the feet of Jesus; instead, I felt like the world's footstool. I was running through life too fast to enjoy it, and even though I was a Christian, I was blinded to the truth that Jesus really was the one and only thing I really needed.

When I eventually reached that "end of the rope" stage and admitted my need for him, I finally discovered the only thing I had needed to do all along to attain the peace I so desired was to ask God for it.

When I finally bowed my head and actually asked, his gentle voice fluttered through my spirit like a crisp fall breeze, and the sensation of serenity literally brought me to my knees—partly because I realized how many years I had wasted seeking stress relief in all the wrong places and partly because I was overwhelmed with the realization of how long God had been waiting for me to give him control. I had finally embraced the promise found in Matthew 21:22, which says, "You can pray for anything, and if you have faith, you will receive it." The only "anything" I wanted was peace.

Since you have chosen to read this particular book instead of all the other books on the shelves, I would dare to assume that you may be feeling sick with stress, just as I was. You may be drowning in a life overcome by busyness, anxiety, and worry. You may be sick and tired of being sick and tired. And you may just be realizing that you have also allowed stress to become your new "normal," too.

So, sweet friend, if this describes you, today is the perfect day to start anew. Today is the perfect day to humble yourself before your Heavenly Father and admit that you have been sick with stress. Today, the doors of God's peace swing open as he gives you a new glimpse into your life. It may be time for you to bow your head, confess that you have allowed stress to overshadow your faith, and admit that you too are one of those sick and imperfect people whom Jesus died for.

Our humility catapults us into the arms of Jesus, where we can allow ourselves to admit that whether or not we feel peace and joy in our hearts is completely, absolutely, unequivocally up to us and us alone. But this all takes time.

After my life-changing God encounter, my prayers became more frequent and consistent. Over a period of time, God slowly began to lead me down a new and mysterious path. A path laced with insight and understanding. A path dependent on faith and trust. A path involving some sacrifice, but one that led me to a place of peace and calmness of spirit I thought was only feasible for people with perfect marriages, perfect children, perfect careers, perfect finances, perfect health, and perfect, problem-free lives. I now know God's peace is available to each and every one of us, regardless of our circumstances.

We are reminded of this promise in John 14:27, when Jesus told his disciples that although he would soon be leaving the world, he was leaving them with a gift: "I am leaving you with a gift—peace of mind and heart. And the peace I give is a gift the world cannot give. So don't be troubled or afraid." In *The Message,* the first half of this same verse reads: "I'm leaving you well and whole. That's my parting gift to you. Peace." What a beautiful gift. And what a shame it is that we choose to let life rob us of such a gift. But there is hope. What a blessing it is that we can reach out and reclaim our gift the very second we choose to do so—and it will be ours.

In Mark 2:17, Jesus said, "Healthy people don't need a doctor— sick people do. I have come to call not those who think they are righteous, but those who know they are sinners." He came to save our souls for eternity, but he also came to save our hearts so we could live a life of peace while on earth rather than live under the burden of stress and anxiety, which is in itself another form of sickness.

Overwhelming stress is as much an illness to our soul as cancer is to our body. Jesus came to heal not those who were sick with physical illnesses, although he did perform many healing miracles, but to heal those who were sick with spiritual illnesses—including the debilitating disease of stress. Our hearts are sick when they are burdened with stress, and Jesus is the eternal healer of hearts. He came to bring peace to those who long for real, lasting serenity, and not merely the temporary peace the world has to offer. He came to bring peace that, from a worldly perspective, is only a fantasy but, through him, can become a reality.

As my journey progressed from the stress zone to the faith zone and made my walk with God a priority again, I allowed God's promises to awaken my spirit. I slowly began to understand *I* was the only person who had control over my mind. *I* was the only person who had authority over the joy in my heart. *I* was the only person who could determine my attitude on any given day. *I* had to choose to be an optimist, despite negative circumstances. *I* had to make a decision to live life on purpose, as God intended, or to just simply be alive. *I* had to choose to trust God had my circumstances under control and was capable of handling my problems. *I* was the only person who could control how stressed I felt, and *I* could no longer blame anyone else.

Even when other people or circumstances were the external cause of stress, only *I* could allow those problems to suffocate my internal peace. Only *I* could grant permission for the flame in my heart to be snuffed out like a candle.

Whatever you are facing, ask God to reveal what the real root causes are for your stress. Ask him for a looking glass glimpse into your life. Is it circumstances, emotions, resentment, bitterness, pain from your past, the hurtful actions of others, or maybe feelings of helplessness or hopelessness? Is it the exhausting task of playing the blame game? Is it wearing a mask that is weighing you down? Have you allowed others to snuff your inner flame? Is it the strain of parenting? Is it addictions to something or someone? Is it the burdens of life, marital problems, parenting challenges, or work? Or is it possibly your perspective about all these things?

Take a moment right now to pause and pray for the strength, courage, desire, and persistence to look deep into your soul and start trying to see the problem for what it really is. Soul searching and spending time in prayer are both effective ways to open our eyes about what changes we need to make in our lives and where the root of our stress lies, but it may take time to discern. It may seem impossible at first, but taking a peek inside our hearts is the first step toward making positive changes in our lives, one stressor at a time.

Why Does It Really Matter If I'm Stressed?

If stress is so prevalent in our world today, should we even attempt to fight it? Is it something that deserves our undivided attention, or is it simply just a sign of the times that we should accept and live with?

Even though stress might be the new normal for our culture, especially in the wake of 2020, it is not the normal God ever intended for us. The COVID-19 pandemic affected every aspect of American life. Even though I feel I'm someone who can handle a lot of pressure well and avoid letting things push me over the edge, even I have gotten to the point where my level of stress and anxiety over the pandemic situation was high. Nine months into this unprecedented experience, I am *so* over it. I'm over my favorite restaurants and hot spots being closed or having limited capacity; over standing in lines; mask wearing; constantly wondering if you've been exposed and then, if you have been exposed, fretting over whether to quarantine or get tested; being restricted from or afraid to be around friends, family, and loved ones; and not even being able to go to my local gym. Then, to make matters worse, the political unrest of our present time could push even the most peace-filled person beyond the point of tolerance. I have often found myself feeling anxious, with my heart racing, simply because of all the stress going on around me that is out of my control, coupled with the normal stressors of everyday life, work, and family. I can only imagine you have shared these same feelings. And even though they are not uncommon, they are not healthy.

In May 2020, the American Psychological Association (APA) conducted its annual Stress in America poll, but adapted it into a monthly analysis of stressors and stress levels. It specifically studied the negative mental health effects of the coronavirus and pointed out emphatically that the physical, emotional, and mental health effects of the pandemic would be serious and long lasting. As fully expected, the study showed that the majority of Americans were experiencing much higher levels of stress than in years past, and stress was already an epidemic in our country prior to 2020!

Parents felt some of the highest stress levels due to the shutdowns of the education system and managing online learning, with most parents saying their stress level was an 8 out of 10. In terms of political affiliation, the way the government responded to the pandemic was a source of significant stress for two-thirds of Republicans and three-fourths of Democrats surveyed. The economy was also reported as a significant source of stress for 70 percent of adults, a huge jump from the 46 percent reported previously.[1] Regardless of the source (and they are countless!), stress is off the chart for the majority of the population and, if left unacknowledged, can have dire consequences.

You see, stress is like a ticking time bomb and, when ignored and not addressed, will eventually result in an emotional implosion—riddling our spirits with virtual bullet holes; destroying our bodies, which are to be God's temples; and scattering emotional shrapnel over every area of our lives. Even though people have learned to adapt to stress as a normal part of life, our bodies are not quite so cooperative.

The damage stress can inflict is seemingly limitless, and continuing to ignore stress not only causes an onslaught of physical problems but also serves as proof that we have not been caring for our bodies as God intended. Even stress eating and stress caused by the consequences of overeating are further evidence of neglecting our duties as caretakers.

Your Body, but God's Temple

One Wednesday evening, I was driving my then sixteen-year-old daughter Morgan to church, and she wanted to go to the Wendy's drive-through. I pulled up to the window to get her a quick bite, and she ordered a Double Baconator Combo—a huge hamburger with two thick patties, six strips of bacon, cheese, all the toppings, plus an oversized fry and a large soft drink. I could never eat a hamburger that big, and I was amazed that, with her 110-pound self, she thought she could. I just assumed that her eyes were bigger than her stomach.

As she dove into the bag, reaching for her hot, delicious-smelling meal, I gently warned her, in my most concerned and loving mom voice, that bad eating habits and fatty foods would eventually catch up to her from a weight perspective, but, more importantly, they were very unhealthy. Then our conversation took an interesting twist.

Just the week before, I had been studying the book of Leviticus, which focuses on the building of God's temple by the Israelites after they had left Egypt, and apparently, I had "temple on the brain" syndrome.

As I continued driving, I took advantage of a teaching moment to remind my daughter that her body was God's temple; therefore, she should take care of it, and part of taking care of it was eating healthy. With her typical teenage smirk at the parental wisdom she was being given, she uttered, "Mom, are you trying to tell me that eating this hamburger is a sin?!"

I laughed, and our comical conversation went on for several more minutes until I dropped her off at church. It wasn't that I had anything against hamburgers, but after having read countless details about the tabernacle (the tent version of the temple), I had recently embraced a newfound appreciation for its sacredness and was encouraged by knowing the Lord actually resided in the temple in biblical times. I admired the hours of work that were devoted to building the tabernacle, and the many rules and requirements God set forth regarding honoring and caring for it.

In the New Testament, we are reminded many times about how we are now God's dwelling place, instead of a tent or building made by the hands of man. We no longer have to worship, pray, or converse with God in a specifically designated place, because as believers, his Spirit lives within us and we are indeed his holy temple.

First Corinthians 3:16–17 says, "Don't you know that you yourselves are God's temple and that God's Spirit lives in you? If anyone destroys God's temple, God will destroy him; for God's temple is sacred, and you are that temple" (NIV).

At first glance, the verses above seem to imply an overwhelming responsibility to understand that we truly are God's temple, that we are the only ones who can take care of it, and that he has commanded us to do just that. But most importantly, he warns us that there are consequences for ignoring this command—consequences that could potentially lead to destruction.

Healthy eating is not the only way we can care for our bodies, but it is an important issue that is often ignored by many. Unfortunately, the society we live in has become accustomed to and even expectant of larger portions, resulting in overeating and the daily consumption of unhealthy, overprocessed, fattening foods, which has led to record levels of obesity in America. In fact, anxiety over the events of 2020 caused a lot of people to adopt many unhealthy coping mechanisms, including "stress eating," which is especially prevalent among women and can lead to obesity and accompanying health issues.

According to a study in September 2020, the obesity rates in America have risen to exceed 35 percent of the population in twelve states, 30 percent in thirty-five states, and 25 percent in forty-eight states.[2] I find it interesting that statistics show that both stress and obesity have increased simultaneously, and I feel confident there is a connection. Although there are many other factors that often play a role in overeating, how a person feels is going to drive their behaviors, and for many people, eating is a way to cope with stress. It's easy to see how this could happen. After all, babies quickly learn that eating makes them feel safe and loved, and God created us to hunger for those sweet emotions. As adults, we still long to have those same emotional needs met, but that longing can turn into trouble if we try to meet our needs with food. When overeating becomes our only way to cope, weight gain is imminent, frustration and self-condemnation kick in, and stress is sure to have yet another excuse to intrude on our lives. Some people may be completely unaware that food has become a stress relief mechanism for them, while others know they have a problem but feel helpless to fix it.

Overeating is only one means of coping with stress that people may struggle with. Drinking, smoking, drugs, undereating, cutting, isolation, overuse of anxiety medications, and more could all be classified as unhealthy ways of trying to deal with stress, all of which will have negative, long-term, and possibly permanent consequences, even when stressors themselves are no longer present.

Living a life plagued by the disease of stress and busyness is not only unhealthy living, bringing with it the potential for serious negative consequences to our physical bodies, but it also carries a looming threat to our hearts and souls as well. Understanding the importance that God places on caring for his temple, our bodies, cannot be overlooked as we begin this journey to discover a "stress-less life."

It matters to God if you are stressed, because he knows stress puts your body, his temple, in great jeopardy, preventing you from living the abundant life he wants you to enjoy. I hope that by the end of this book, you will see why this should matter to you, too.

From Expert to Experienced

I worked at an accounting firm for many years, and one of my main responsibilities was corporate training. I spent several years traveling the southeastern United States, conducting training sessions for firm employees. Despite feeling stressed, maxed out, burnt out, and overwhelmed trying to juggle my career, marriage, and motherhood, along with a variety of unexplainable health problems, I dove headfirst into my training responsibilities but eventually found myself immersed deep in chaos and stress, in way over my head, emotionally and physically spent. Even every breath felt like a chore. After finally getting fed up and resigning from that position, I took a job as a freelance corporate trainer and often taught workshops on the topic of stress management. Over time, I became an expert on the topic—from an informational corporate standpoint, of course.

My knowledge continued to grow about all the *right* things to teach employees who were stressed. I knew what activities to recommend to promote tranquility at home and work. I knew all the best breathing techniques, muscle relaxation exercises, and peace-inducing meditation strategies. I knew the best-selling stress management books to recommend, the most popular websites offering great tips for dealing with stress, and what type of music was most soothing for the heart, mind, and soul.

I was well-versed in all the suggestions to help strengthen strained relationships between coworkers and management, build stronger teams, and reduce stress and anxiety among team members.

You see, I was trained in all the *worldly* ways to deal with stress. Oh yes, this former stress poster child had become a Stress Management Expert, and I had *all* the answers. Or so I thought.

Trust me when I say that even though I had left my full-time, stressful career behind, my life was still full of stressors. The stress that had been removed from my ten-hour workday was quickly replaced with financial issues, parenting challenges, marital problems, worry over sick family members, and an array of newfound stressors. The irony was that in the midst of my stress-expert, corporate-training career of teaching the how-tos, dos, and don'ts of dealing with stress, I had once again become the National Poster Child for the Most Frazzled Woman of the Year.

Instead of becoming an expert on stress management in my own life, I had become an expert on using Band-Aids to cover up my on-edge lifestyle, while giving the illusion that I had it all together. Although I was devoted to teaching other people about controlling their stress through worldly measures, I knew full well I wasn't applying any of them in my own life.

But, even worse, I secretly knew that in addition to not practicing the techniques I was preaching to the secular world, and the fact that my health was failing for reasons I couldn't explain at the time, I was also failing to seek peace through my Savior. Rather than turning to God for answers, I turned back to blaming others. Once again, I became sure that it was not my fault I was stressed, it was still everyone else's fault! I was convinced I had a right and an obligation to blame my hurt and stress on whomever or whatever was causing it.

But, as God continued to work on my burdened heart, he slowly began to chisel away at my invisible mask of fakeness, opening up my spirit so he could shine through. Once again, I found myself hanging on to the end of my rope. I bowed my head and ashamedly admitted to God that I had again allowed myself to get pulled into a life consumed by chaos and fallen back into the blame game. I had yet again let the worries of the world blind me to the peace available in him and the fact that he could handle it all. I needed him to rescue me from myself and my stress, and when I called out in prayer, my Rescuer came through, yet again, as he always so faithfully does.

I sensed a sudden change in my spirit, and I knew my heart was on the brink of being transformed. God had been waiting patiently for me to see that only he held the answers to the inner peace I was so desperately searching for. He had been waiting for me to seek him and had given me more than sufficient time to discover that all the worldly ways of managing stress I had been teaching were completely useless. They were feel-good-in-the-moment techniques, not life-changing tools. They could bring temporary relaxation but could never bring permanent peace.

I simply had been too stressed to listen to God. But now that I was listening, I embraced the realization that I had the potential, in him and through him, to once and for all overcome the stronghold stress had held over my life for far too long. Without a shadow of doubt, I now knew I needed to focus on making his peace the pattern of my life instead of living in a pattern of constantly falling in and out of the stress pit every time I experienced life's ups and downs. When true faith and trust in my Savior became a reality in my heart, living less stressed became a reality in my life. It didn't happen overnight, but it did happen. And it can happen for you, too.

When I finally began to assume responsibility for my own actions and feelings and resumed authority over my emotions. I realized most of my stress was rooted in trying to control circumstances I had no control over. This realization freed me from trying to change people I couldn't change, from attempting to fix things I had no resources to fix, from focusing on the unfairness of life instead of the blessings I had been given, and from worrying over problems I had no power to remedy. I was wasting infinite amounts of time, energy, and emotion on things that were completely, 101 percent, out of my control!

So if the truth be known, all my stress was really self-induced; and in all honesty, that is the case for most people—and possibly the case for you. I would be remiss if I failed to acknowledge what you might be thinking right now, after implying your stress is your own fault: *What the what? No way! That person / circumstance / wrongdoing / unfairness / hardship / adversity / illness / money problem / job*

/ boss is the cause of my stress! How dare you insinuate I am bringing this anxiety on myself! The nerve of you, Tracie! (Slams book closed.)

Friend, I absolutely understand if you disagree completely and adamantly with the idea that your stress is even partly your fault. Maybe you cannot imagine relinquishing blame for other people or circumstances and taking ownership of your own state of mind. Maybe you truly believe to the depths of your soul the actions of other people are the root cause of your stress or the difficult situations in your life, which are not even your fault, are the real culprits. And those feelings are completely and absolutely valid. I would never negate your deepest raw emotions because those feelings are real. When we have been hurt by people or by life, or when circumstances are difficult and painful, it's hard to release blame. We feel like we are letting those people or circumstances off the hook, and they don't deserve that type of grace. It's hard to push past our emotions and latch onto faith when our hearts are heavy, anxiety is high, and we feel helpless to escape those feelings.

I know it's hard, but it can be done, and it is so worth it.

As you continue to read through this book, my prayer is you will learn to understand and believe without a shadow of a doubt that despite your valid emotions, raw feelings, open wounds, and heavy heart, and no matter what your stressors are, *you* are the only one who has authority over your attitude, your joy, your stress level, and your peace.

The Search for Serenity

The Serenity Prayer is a common prayer, known to most believers and nonbelievers alike. This prayer was originally a simple, untitled prayer that historically has been dated back as early as 1936 and is credited to a theologian named Reinhold Niebuhr. Niebuhr's prayer goes like this:

> *God grant me the serenity*
> *to accept the things I cannot change;*
> *courage to change the things I can;*
> *and wisdom to know the difference.*

Sounds easy enough right? I wish I had practiced this art of acceptance when I was stressed to the max from trying to control things I couldn't change. But there is nothing easy about finding serenity, and I know I am not alone in that struggle. Millions of people fall prey to this trap every day and fail to see the difference between what they can change and what they *cannot.* Instead of seeking relief from their stress by focusing on the things within their power to change, they spin their wheels, obsessing over problems that are out of their control. As a result, they abandon the possibility of peace, resigning themselves to living in perpetual chaos, simply because they don't believe life can, or should, be different. It's a universal epidemic of abnormal proportions.

Living a life devoid of stress seems so foreign and impossible to most people that they don't even attempt to figure out how to fix the problem, especially in today's chaotic world. Instead, most people just surrender to living in the prison of stress they have come to believe is their fate. It has become normal, and people accept it as normal, but it's not how God intended for us to live. Yet our accepting of stress as normal and never committing to change is the primary reason doctors' offices are flooded with scores of patients every day complaining about a myriad of ailments and diseases, painfully unaware their problems are rooted in stress-related factors. (We'll delve deeper into a discussion of the health risks of stress in Chapter Two, and you may want to prepare for a real eye-opener!)

This serenity prayer epitomizes the idea that the remedy for stress starts in the mind. If we can't change something, or someone, why do we waste time and energy trying to make change happen? If we have no power to change a circumstance or person, then every effort to force a change to occur will be futile. And with each additional futile effort, anxiety builds and stress intensifies.

I came across another rendition of the Serenity Prayer that I liked even more than the first. A philosopher named W. W. Bartley wrote it, and his version goes like this:

> *For every ailment under the sun*
> *There is a remedy, or there is none;*
> *If there be one, try to find it;*
> *If there be none, never mind it.*

It has the same concept as the others but with a different spin on it—if you can't fix it yourself, never mind it! Put it in God's hands, and let him do the work. To use the old familiar cliché, let go and let God! When we finally surrender to God instead of stress and trust that he has everything under control, the vicious cycle of stress can come to a screeching halt, which opens the door for God to finally begin to do his work.

If we could change the stress in our lives with the wave of a magic wand, we certainly would; but the reality is that another stressor would surely follow right along behind it. If there is one consistent thing about problems, it would be that they consistently pop up! Stressful events can happen every day. Life is always going to be busy, so trying to find out how life can be completely stress-free would be a pointless and unrewarding journey. This is why it is so important that we learn how to recognize and manage our stress and intentionally ask for God's peace every single morning when we arise.

We *can* find peace and joy by learning to control our stress instead of letting it control us. This change will begin to emerge when we focus our energies in the right place and realize we need to change our attitudes about our stress and realize we don't have to live under the toxicity of anxiety. Stress typically does not come from the situations in our lives but rather from the ways we handle those situations.

Believe it or not, I came across a third version of the Serenity Prayer that resonated with me even more than the other two. It reads like this:

> *God grant me the serenity*
> *to accept the people I cannot change,*
> *the courage to change the only person I can,*
> *and the wisdom to know that person is me.*
> (author unknown)

True and meaningful change begins from the inside out, and not the other way around. Change has to begin with ourselves, and that takes courage.

The First Step to Freedom

I have witnessed God's power over stress, and I now fully believe we all have complete control over whether we spend life stressed, frazzled, overwhelmed, and depressed, or happy, at peace, and fulfilled, despite the circumstances we face. And truth be told, not all stressful circumstances are bad, although we often think they are. Sometimes the things that stress us out are actually good things.

Think of some typical negative issues we know cause stress: Finances. Poor economy. Poverty. Government. Bankruptcy. News headlines. Cancer. Chronic illnesses. Terminal illnesses. Funerals. Abuse. Betrayal. Job loss. Job frustration. Drug or alcohol addiction. Home foreclosures. Difficult supervisors. Hurtful coworkers. Backstabbing. Office politics. Divorce. Family problems. Parenting. Teenagers. Housework. Bills. Personal safety. Politics. Death. Natural disasters. War. But positive and wonderful situations can also cause stress: Think weddings. New babies. New jobs. New relationships. Old relationships. Crime. Job relocations. Holidays.

Birthdays. These are merely a few examples of the good and bad situations we face each and every day, all while not even batting an eye to the stress they can cause to course through our veins.

Whether we are experiencing "good" stressful situations or "bad" ones, the physical, emotional, and mental consequences of stress can be exactly the same. Our bodies cannot determine what type of stress we are encountering, just that our emotions are out of whack. So, since stress in every form is here to stay, what we must realize is that it is not the stressful situations in and of themselves that cause our stress but the way we process and handle those stressful situations.

Just because stress is here to stay doesn't mean we are doomed to become its victims. We have the power to fight it by finding courage in God but also by recognizing our body's red flags. We need to live in a state of awareness of what our bodies are trying to tell us.

The worst health consequences of extreme and overwhelming stress begin when basic symptoms are overlooked or when people choose to deliberately ignore their stress, thinking it won't matter. But the reality is that "stress is a major contributing factor either directly or indirectly, to coronary artery disease, cancer, respiratory disorders, accidental injuries, cirrhosis of the liver and suicide; the six leading causes of death in the United States. Stress aggravates other conditions such as multiple sclerosis, diabetes, herpes, mental illness, alcoholism, drug abuse, and family discord and violence."[3] This information came as an absolute shock to me. We have all heard stress is not good for us, but rarely do we hear it can actually end life as we know it. Never have I read an obituary in the newspaper listing the cause of death as "stress." But, because stress is considered normal for our society, people overlook the damage it can cause. They ignore minor health problems until they turn into bigger health problems, often never recognizing their stress was the actual root cause of the medical issue.

Stress has always been a major problem in the United States, but needless to say, 2020 stress levels were off the charts, to the point of being called a national mental health crisis—and this trend has continued into 2021. As noted previously, every year since 2007, the American Psychological Association (APA) has surveyed US citizens about their stress levels and how they are dealing with stress in their lives, both mentally and physically. Over the past fourteen years, the APA has rated how various external factors happening in our country have negatively affected people's stress levels, always documenting that a large majority of people were experiencing high levels of stress.

As for 2020? We're in a whole new ballgame, sister. The APA study revealed that while Americans were still experiencing stress from the normal factors of life that had always been present in previous years, these issues were now compounded by the stress of the COVID-19 pandemic. In fact, nearly 8 in 10 adults (78 percent) say the pandemic is a significant source of stress in their lives. And 2 in 3 adults (67 percent) say they have experienced increased stress over the course of the pandemic, to the point where they admittedly say their physical and emotional symptoms of stress are obvious—increased tension felt in their bodies, snapping or getting angry quickly, unexpected mood swings, or screaming or yelling at loved ones.[4] I can certainly relate. Can you?

Not only do we still have to bear the stress of our normal personal lives, along with alarming daily reports from news channels of crime, economic failure, job loss, unemployment, mass shootings, global warming, and more, but now we're facing a pandemic? As of October 2020, the death toll from coronavirus topped 215,000 in the United States—more than the number of Americans who died in World War I, the Vietnam War, and the Korean War combined.[5] How could that not stress you out? Just the sheer numbers we hear in these reports and on the news cause fear and worry to burn in our minds, like lighter fluid fueling the stress in our hearts.

It can all become too much for anyone. And, for some, stress can turn fatal if they don't recognize it and get it under control. It truly is a silent killer—but fortunately we have the cure in our power. We can't change everything *around* us, but we can change everything *within* us.

I know full well when I'm stressed to an unhealthy level. My heart is racing, I'm anxious, I start feeling spaced out, like I can't keep my thoughts straight, and my hands might even shake. I have found myself reaching that point countless times, whether it's from simply feeling overwhelmed and overloaded at work, to relationship problems out of my control to fix, to fretting over the chaos of events happening in our world. At times, I keep pushing forward, thinking, *I got this.* But, eventually, it gets me instead. I've learned that forcing myself to tap into my own willpower to make changes—to do whatever it takes to minimize my stress, whether in the moment or for the long haul—is a move that could literally save or extend my life.

Simply put, most Americans know they are stressed and that their stress is negatively affecting their health, but they don't have the courage, willingness, or knowledge to implement positive changes in their lives.

And therein lies part of the problem—a lack of willpower to change. We know we need the willpower to lose those extra ten pounds we packed on (maybe during quarantine!) or to make ourselves go to the gym every day. Willpower is the determining factor between success and failure in any aspect of life; and we also need willpower to manage our stress. We have to first realize how much we *need to*, and then build up our willpower to create our *want to*.

The problem is that it's a catch-22. Stress affects our decision-making, zaps our energy, and depletes our willpower to do what's healthy for our hearts, minds, and bodies.[6] When we're super stressed, our energy levels are lower and the brainpower we need to use to focus on making healthy choices or doing something to eliminate our stress gets pulled in a different direction.

It is believed, based on survey results, that a lack of willpower to change is one of the top challenges for most people: "Americans cite lack of willpower as the biggest barrier to adopting healthier behavior. But 70 percent believe that willpower is something they can learn or improve—if only they had more money, energy or confidence in their ability to change."[7]

Stress is obviously something many people try to ignore, but it is nothing to mess around with, and blaming it all on a lack of willpower is a pretty poor excuse. Willpower comes when there is sufficient information to signify that a change is crucial. The motivation to change can come from Matthew 19:26, where we are reminded that all things are possible with God.

If you care about your health, your life, your loved ones, your future, and even your walk with Christ, today is the perfect day to admit your need for help. To stop blaming a lack of willpower, blaming other people, or living with the mindset that you are at the mercy of your circumstances. Instead, start by taking a hard look at your mind, spirit, and body, acknowledging any symptoms of stress you may have been ignoring, and make a commitment to yourself to change. You have the power, and the willpower, to change—if you want it bad enough.

○⌇ Reflection Questions

1. Have you been habitually blaming people and circumstances for your stress? Make a list of the people or circumstances you have been attributing blame to. Ask God to help you see things from his perspective, and seek his strength to release other people from responsibility for your stress.

2. What Band-Aids have you been using to deal with your stress? Have these Band-Aids been helpful or harmful?

3. How would you finish this statement:

"If _____, *I wouldn't be stressed."*
Write out all of your *"if"* statements that come to mind.

4. Have the problems you listed above caused you to overlook or discount your blessings? Make a list of blessings you may have taken for granted, and spend time in prayer expressing praise and gratitude to God for them. Thank God for the difficult circumstances you are in as well, trusting that, in some way, he will use them for his greater purposes. Surrender them to him and let him worry about the outcomes, so you can live stress-free.

5. Has stress become your "new normal"? To help clarify this concept, draw two columns on a piece of paper and do the following: In column one, write out a few descriptive words that signify the "normal" you would like to have (or what used to be normal for you). In column two, write a few words that describe your current normal. Consider the differences, and pray for God to help you see how you can begin making strides to get back to your old normal (for example, responsibilities that you can let go of, stressors you can walk away from, ways to strengthen your faith and find the ability to persevere, people who can support you, etc.).

6. Have you ever really asked God for peace and expected to receive it? If yes, reminisce about how you felt when God granted you peace in the midst of a difficult situation. Jot down the emotions and thoughts that come to mind. Then pray and ask God to allow that sweet memory to be fuel for your faith as you face new stressors. If your answer is no, get on your knees today and ask God for this priceless gift of peace and then believe that he will provide it.

7. What can you do today to begin assuming responsibility for your stress?

Stress-Busting Scriptures

I have set the LORD always before me.
Because he is at my right hand, I will not be shaken.

Psalm 16:8 NIV

❧

Cast your cares on the LORD and he will sustain you;
he will never let the righteous fall.

Psalm 55:22 NIV

❧

In my distress I called to the LORD; I called out to my God.
From his temple he heard my voice; my cry came to his ears.

2 Samuel 22:7 NIV

❧

The LORD hears his people when they call to him for help.
He rescues them from all their troubles.

Psalm 34:17

❧

Don't be afraid, for I am with you.
Don't be discouraged, for I am your God.
I will strengthen you and help you.
I will hold you up with my victorious right hand.

Isaiah 41:10

❧

CHAPTER TWO

Does It Really Matter If I'm Stressed Out?

Stress typically doesn't happen overnight. Though an unexpected or tragic situation can spontaneously rage into our lives causing immediate stress and worry, it normally takes a period of time for stress to reach its full potential. Any situation or circumstance, whether good or bad (as noted previously), can cause varying levels of stress, so figuring out what stresses us most is a key factor in the mission toward a harmonious life and better health—bringing us one step closer to getting a taste of the sweet, peace-filled life we crave.

In the same way a doctor can't prescribe a treatment for your illness until he knows what the illness is, we can't address our own struggle with stress until we know what is actually causing the problem. The stress itself does not need to be the focus, because that is merely the external manifestation of the internal problem. Instead, we need to identify the cause of the stress by doing an in-depth self-assessment of our raw emotions. I realize that right now our entire world is experiencing unprecedented circumstances, and that alone has ushered in a whole new list of stressors for everyone. However, in many cases, our stress most often comes from something that seems to be part of our normal, so we think we just have to deal with it and keep pushing forward, despite the toll it is taking on us. We feel like victims to our circumstances and our stress, unable to escape to a place where our hearts, minds, and bodies can rest.

For example, we may not realize that every time we have to deal with a certain person, our blood pressure rises and our heart races. We may not realize a particular task at work causes us to feel anxious and overwhelmed each time we have to tackle it. We may be unaware we are yet again subconsciously worrying about a situation we thought we had under control. This has happened to me occasionally, when I didn't realize how stressed I was over something until my stomach began having serious issues or my head started pounding. Only when the external symptoms showed up did I realize that internal anxieties had been bubbling under the surface. Our bodies will always tell us what our minds try to ignore.

Recognize Your Personal Stressors

Determining your stressors takes a personal commitment to being in tune with your body and feelings, because what is stressful for another person may not be stressful for you at all, and vice versa. Case in point, some people love to speak in front of groups, while others turn pale faced and get weak in the knees just thinking about it. Some people enjoy working under deadlines and are more productive when pressured, while others may get so tense under pressure they can't even think straight. Some people love spending time with family members, while others would rather have their toes stomped on repeatedly with six-inch high heels than go to a family gathering. Some people know exactly how to comfort someone who is hurting, while others are at a loss for words and break out in a cold sweat during the awkward silence. Some people are motivated by change and can always roll with the punches, while others become mentally paralyzed when change is introduced. Some people love going to parties and social gatherings, while others would rather take an ice bath than have to meet new people.

God made each of us unique. Therefore, no two people are alike in their feelings. As a result, no two people will ever experience, endure, be affected by, or manage stress the same way either, which only further proves why it is so important to know whether you are more vulnerable to stress than other people and know exactly how your body reacts, and this answer lies in your personality type.

For example, people who are high-strung, impatient, and ambitious, may be more at risk for anxiety and experiencing stress-related physical problems because they will frequently push themselves to the breaking point to accomplish their goals at all costs. On the other hand, someone who is more laid back and passive may not get stressed at all, even when faced with the possibility of falling short of meeting his or her expectations, or those of someone else. A couple of other things to consider are that there are certain occupations that may be more stressful than others. And sometimes family history can play a role in determining a person's ability to handle stress, such as if there are any mental illnesses in the family, a history of depression, or if the person grew up in a household that was in a constant state of stress, resulting in the mind being trained to be on stress alert and on guard all the time.

But regardless of your personality, occupation, family history, or whether you are more prone to stress than the next person, the fact remains that too much stress can be dangerous, and the damage of stress does not play favorites.

Self-Assessment

Before we go any further, I want you to take this opportunity to begin thinking about the major stressors in your life. In order to embark on the journey of turning your stressors over to God and letting him replace them with peace, the first step is figuring out exactly what those stressors really are for you.

Take a few moments to fill out the following table. Think about all the people, problems, and circumstances in your life that are causing you stress right now, including anything going on in our country or world that makes your heart beat faster when you think about them. Don't get stressed making your list! But know it's crucial to identify the source of the problem so you can start making strides toward a better life and a better you.

Although this self-assessment/life examination may not be a fun task, it is necessary if you seriously desire to overcome your stress and begin to heal and grow. You may think you already know what your biggest stressors are, but the possibility exists that some problems and harmful emotions have been working overtime in your spirit, yet going unnoticed. So pray before you begin and ask God to open your eyes to issues you may not have thought of before that are stealing your peace and joy. Ask him to help you see things in a new perspective and for this exercise to truly be one that will jump-start you on the road to stress recovery.

Once you are done, follow the instructions in the paragraph after the assessment.

Personal Stress Self-Assessment

The Stressor or Problem?	How Does This Problem Make Me Feel, Physically and Emotionally?	How Is the Problem Affecting My Life?	Do I Have the Ability to Change This Problem?	What Can I Do Differently to Stop Stressing over This?

Now, take a look at your list. Pause and pray over each and every one of the issues that you listed above, and if you haven't already, really give some thought to what you can do differently to stop stressing over those problems or stressors that you have no control over and no power to change. That is simply wasted mental and emotional energy, which drains you physically! Also, be sure you answered honestly about whether or not you have any control over the problem. If you do not, admit whether you have been trying to fix or control the outcome on your own. Ask God to grant you the courage and strength to let those problems go, and let him take over. If other problems come to mind later, come back to this page or your own journal and jot them down as well so you will have a record of everything you are turning over to God.

Close this reflection activity by praying the prayer below or by pouring your heart out to God in your own words.

Dear Heavenly Father, I know you are sovereign and almighty, and I ask for your hand to be upon my life. I am in much need of your strength, wisdom, discernment, and courage to help me deal with these difficult situations or people in my life. I need your guidance and I desire to lay these stressors at your feet and ask for not only your willpower but your strength to do so. Help me to seek out your ways and your desires each morning when I awake, instead of trudging through my days in the same manner I have always done. Equip me with perseverance in my quest to fully trust in you with all of my problems. Please fill my heart with a peace that surpasses all understanding, and lead me into a closer relationship with you as I progress through this book. In Jesus's name I pray, amen.

A Matter of Life and Death

While employed at the accounting firm I have already mentioned, I not only experienced stress; I experienced the destructive consequences of full-blown stress sickness. Although it appeared to be a great career with a successful organization, it demanded a high tolerance for unrelenting stress, which is actually where the idea for this book in your hands was born.

With the hour-long commute, the deadlines, the rampant office politics, the demanding and demeaning boss, the cutthroat tactics, the workload, the worry, the overtime, the frustration, the travel, compounded by the responsibility of three small children, mommy guilt, a difficult marriage, maintaining house and home, and extended family concerns, I had, over time, become one overwhelmed, overcommitted, overstressed, overfrazzled, burnt-out young woman.

I knew deep in my heart something was wrong, but since everyone in my firm lived and worked under the same amount of stress, I honestly thought it was normal. And expected. I assumed if an employee wasn't stressed to the point of losing it, then clearly they weren't doing their job. However, my opinion gradually changed as I grasped the realization that I was not only miserable and unhappy, but oddly experiencing a myriad of unexpected, unexplained, and bothersome health issues, which I had never dealt with before.

I was only in my thirties at the time and the picture of health, so I just didn't understand at the time why my body was turning against me. I had no idea my out-of-control stress level was to blame and was taking a huge physical toll on every part of my being.

The first of many issues I began noticing was consistent blurry vision, which prompted me to visit the eye doctor. I had always been blessed with excellent eyesight and had never worn glasses or contacts, so this strange and rather sudden issue with my vision was highly unusual. I was confident I needed bifocals at an early age, but even after repeated visits, the optometrist continued to assure me that my vision was near perfect. In my frustration, I pondered the possibility that maybe my chosen optometrist had finished last in his graduating class, since he was continually unable to diagnose my obvious onset of partial blindness.

The second problem was a little more serious. Because of ongoing heart palpitations, I began to get a little concerned. I eventually contacted a cardiologist, who performed EKG tests, various blood work, and a couple of heart ultrasounds. I even wore a heart monitor for a few weeks in an attempt to catch my unusual heart activity on tape, and I felt sure I was a prime candidate to keel over of a heart attack at my desk any day. The irregular heartbeats and unusually hard pounding in my chest, at times even hard enough to wake me from a deep sleep in the middle of the night, began to frighten me. My lungs frequently felt restricted, as if a fifty-pound boulder had taken up residence on my chest, making it feel like I could never fully fill my lungs with a fresh breath of air. But just like the optometrist, the cardiologist could find nothing medically wrong with my heart or my lungs.

If those issues weren't bad enough, I also began suffering from severe gastrointestinal problems, including constant diarrhea, stomach cramps, and irregular bathroom habits, thus landing me at the gastroenterologist and the colon doctor. A stomach ulcer was suspected but not found, and all other tests came back void as well. So it was concluded I could possibly have irritable bowel syndrome (IBS)—basically, the doctors couldn't find anything else to blame my symptoms on. I was given a weak prescription and some generic suggestions on how to manage my issues through diet.

To make matters worse, I was practically overdosing on acetaminophen every day as I tried to manage my chronic headaches. I found myself wondering if taking such a large volume of over-the-counter medications was what was causing me to be so forgetful, because I couldn't seem to remember a thing. And I won't even go into my pathetic sleep habits, and how every night I slept like a baby . . . with colic.

Despite my persistent attempts for more than a year to find something, anything, medically wrong with me, the doctors could find no physical evidence of any serious medical concern. I know it sounds like I was just a crazy hypochondriac looking for problems that weren't there, but, you see, it wasn't that I wanted something to be wrong with me—no one hopes to have medical problems. But I was completely unaware that all my external problems, which made me feel like my body was falling apart, were merely symptoms of the internal spiritual problems that no doctor had the wisdom to diagnose.

I had yet to figure out that what I really needed was a cure for my stress. Instead, I desperately wanted someone to help me find a solution, but, since no concrete answers could be found, my physical health continued to decline. I desperately wanted to feel better again. I just wanted my life back. I wanted peace. I wanted joy. I wanted to be happy. But when answers evaded doctors and relief never came, I conceded that change was hopeless. I just needed to accept that these health nuisances were now my new normal, even though I didn't understand them. I had to put on my big girl panties and learn to live with them.

All that time, I was clueless that my out-of-control stress level was the culprit for all my health problems, from the smallest ones to the biggest. I was unaware I was the one bringing destruction upon my own body. Yet what was worse than overlooking the toll stress was taking on my body was overlooking the toll it was taking on my heart. And to be perfectly honest, I didn't even know what real peace looked like anymore.

Peace Can Mean Different Things

There are many ways to define peace, and each one of us may hold a different variation from everyone else. For example, peace to a mom of several young toddlers might be a lack of noise. Peace to a busy employee would be a day without problems or deadlines. Peace to a high school student might be the absence of a bully who taunts him or her every day. Peace to a person struggling financially would mean knowing that all the bills are paid. Peace to a wife whose marriage is in turmoil is going one night without an argument. Peace to a woman whose husband walked out on her and her children is knowing the bills are paid for at least one more month before she has to worry again.

Peace means different things to different people in different seasons of life. But where we must look to find that peace is the common denominator we all share: our sweet Jesus.

Many people think the definition of peace is simply the absence of conflict, but the absence of conflict is only a temporary situation that will eventually come to a close. It is a fragile view of peace, because the peace desired is based solely on one's circumstances.

A much better definition of peace is one that rests on the ability to rise above our circumstances, overcome our innate tendency to stress out over problems, and learn to remain calm and confident despite what is going on around us. That is real peace—a peace based on Christ, not on people or circumstances. A peace based on faith, not on personal desires being met. A peace based on a quieted heart, not on a quiet house. A peace based on the love of Jesus, not on an easy day at work. A peace based on trusting God in all things, not just the easy things we can handle with no problem. A peace that is present in our hearts, even when our entire life is overflowing with chaos. That is the kind of peace only Jesus can give, and once we get a taste of that kind of peace, we are never the same again.

Although Jesus is the Prince of Peace, his life was a far cry from being stress-free. Obviously, the crucifixion was the most stressful day of his life, but he actually experienced and dealt with unrelenting stress each and every day until his earthly life ended and he ascended into heaven to sit at the right hand of his Father.

The biggest difference between the stress Jesus faced and the stress we face is he was better equipped to handle it, as God's son. The fact that he was sinless and pure certainly helped with his reactions, but he still had to manage the human emotions that were present in his human form. The shortest verse in the Bible is John

11:35: "Jesus wept" (NIV). These two words alone prove that Jesus felt strong emotions and stress was a part of his life. His words and actions speak volumes for how we can handle the stress in our own lives, through the strength and wisdom he willingly offers, if we choose to use our willpower to fight the battle against stress—the battle for our own peace, health, and happiness.

Questions

1. Do you feel like a ticking time bomb? What situations are causing you to feel that way today?

2. What changes could you implement in your life to begin taking better care of yourself, God's temple? Consider inviting a friend to join you in your journey to live healthier and less stressed. Share your personal commitments for change so you can hold each other accountable and offer support and encouragement to meet your goals.

3. What are some of your biggest personal stressors? In what ways can you prepare in advance to avoid getting upset by them in the future?

4. Have you been experiencing any physical problems that could be rooted in stress? If so, list them below.

5. If you listed some symptoms above, ask yourself whether you have been ignoring them or possibly attributing them to something other than stress-related factors.

6. Consider whether any of your symptoms could be endangering your overall health. Are there any changes that need to be made in your life so that stress doesn't damage your long-term health and life span?

7. Is it possible that your stress has created a barrier between you and God? If your answer is yes, have a conversation with God about it, and write out your prayer below, or consider praying this prayer:

Dear Lord, I never realized that ignoring my stress signified I didn't care about my body, your temple. I simply never considered the fact that my stress could take such a huge toll on me physically. Ashamedly, I also never recognized the toll it was taking on me spiritually. I ask for your forgiveness for allowing my stressful circumstances to pull me away from you, instead of pushing me toward you. I am beginning to see that, though I have been blinded to it until now, stress is a bigger problem in my life than I once thought. Jesus, please fill me with peace and assurance that you are with me. Empower me through your Spirit to take a stand for my health, my family, my future, and my faith and to persevere in whatever it takes to gain control of my life again. Walk beside me as I embark on this journey to be less stressed and as I open my spiritual eyes to see and feel you at work, especially on the hardest of days. In Jesus's name, amen.

Stress-Busting Scriptures

My son, pay attention to what I say; listen closely to my words. Do not let them out of your sight, keep them within your heart; for they are life to those who find them and health to a man's whole body.

Proverbs 4:20–22 NIV

༈

Then they cried to the LORD in their trouble, and he saved them from their distress. He sent forth his word and healed them; he rescued them from the grave. Let them give thanks to the LORD for his unfailing love and his wonderful deeds for men.

Psalm 107:19–21 NIV

༈

So don't worry about these things, saying, "What will we eat? What will we drink? What will we wear?" These things dominate the thoughts of unbelievers, but your heavenly Father already knows all your needs. Seek the Kingdom of God above all else, and live righteously, and he will give you everything you need. So don't worry about tomorrow, for tomorrow will bring its own worries. Today's trouble is enough for today.

Matthew 6:31–34

༈

I am leaving you with a gift—peace of mind and heart. And the peace I give is a gift the world cannot give. So don't be troubled or afraid.

John 14:27

༈

I have told you all this so that you may have peace in me. Here on earth you will have many trials and sorrows. But take heart, because I have overcome the world.

John 16:33

༈

CHAPTER THREE

The Silent Killer

No doubt about it—stress can kill. If it doesn't kill us, it will absolutely leave its mark.

Stress is a chronic disease that is rampant in today's society, and as noted previously, it is gradually morphing into a national mental illness epidemic due to the excessive amount of stressors present in our world today—most, if not all, we have no power over. If multiple studies, year after year, consistently show stress is a growing problem in our nation, regardless of age, sex, or race, then why do most of us accept stress as normal and intentionally ignore its consequences?

Consider this: If you found out you had cancer, would you refuse treatment that might save your life? Of course not! Likewise, if you know you are stressed to an unhealthy level yet refuse to implement necessary changes to help eliminate or reduce your stress, then you are, in essence, refusing treatment and jeopardizing your own life. Stress is nothing to mess around with.

Mind over Matter

Most emotional and physical symptoms of stress and depression are not typically caused by the circumstances themselves, but instead by how our minds perceive what is going on and how our hearts hold up under pressure. The physical damage stress can inflict on our bodies is unsettling, but it can also wreak havoc on us mentally.

Alarmingly, women are becoming victims of stress even more than men, primarily because of stress over the economy and finances. Currently, there are six million women who are struggling with depression. Not that stress is the only factor that causes depression, but there is a proven link.

A doctor from the Mayo Clinic wrote an online article about how chronic stress can increase the risk of developing depression, especially for people who do not use the proper coping methods or acknowledge their need for stress reduction. He confirmed that stress itself isn't abnormal, but the way we deal with stress can undermine our long-term health. If left unmanaged, chronic stress can lead to frequent bad moods, strained relationships, and possibly even the inability to carry out normal daily routines—all of which can begin a dangerous downward spiral toward clinical depression.[8]

So friend, do you still think stress doesn't matter? I hope your eyes have been opened to the physical and mental risks you are taking when you choose to ignore your stress. How amazing might you feel if you finally made the commitment to stop the vicious cycle of stress in your life and start taking back your life, health, and happiness before it's too late? Think about it.

Discovering the Great Physician

It pains me to think of the number of times I needed the healing of God's powerful hands but instead sought out attention from doctors or tried to rid myself of issues through self-diagnoses, medications, and sleep. What a shame that when we find ourselves in the most desperate of situations, we are too stubborn to ask God for healing until we get to that "end-of-our-rope" stage. Granted, there are times when we need to seek out medical advice, but there are also times when we need to seek out holy intervention instead.

Jesus is often referred to as "the Great Physician," but typically when people use this term, they are praying for physical healing for a loved one or for themselves. Although praying for physical healing is important and necessary, we already know Jesus walked the earth to provide something even more important than physical healing. He came bringing spiritual healing that not only saves the soul but saturates it with peace and minimizes the stress in our hearts.

I love the way Psalm 103:2–5 reminds us of this saving grace: "Let all that I am praise the LORD; may I never forget the good things he does for me. He forgives all my sins and heals all my diseases. He redeems me from death and crowns me with love and tender mercies. He fills my life with good things. My youth is renewed like the eagle's!"

The reason Christ came to earth was because we needed him, now and eternally. God knew we would one day find ourselves in a pit, whether deep or shallow, and that we would all need to be redeemed by his love and renewed in our spirits. God also knew just how much we needed a Great Physician, and out of compassion for us he sent his son Jesus to fill that role. In order to tap into his healing power and find peace, we simply have to seek him first—above all else. Above practical strategies and tips for stress management. Above lengthy yoga sessions. Above breathing and relaxation exercises. Above shopping therapy. Above bubble baths. Above all else.

But let's face it, unfortunately, our typical way of handling stress is not to put God above all else. In fact, it seems sometimes we tend to view God like the Red Cross—someone to call upon when we are in grave, unexpected, or seemingly hopeless crisis situations. We often see him as someone to look to for help only when we have exhausted all other options. Yet God's desire is to be a part of our lives in the good and bad times, when we are stressed and when we are not. He wants to be our first responder, not our last resort, and he came to heal those who are sick in heart, not just sick in body.

I thought I knew the epitome of stress from my experience at the accounting firm, but when my marriage of twenty-five years fell apart, stress took on an entirely new level. I found myself pleading for God's intervention. The reality of what I was facing opened the door for overwhelming stress to come raging through my heart, mind, and body, as if they all had been rammed with the force of a fast-moving freight train.

I prayed and cried for weeks and months on end. I consistently asked God for a peace that deep down I didn't believe was possible, considering the heartbreak, fear, and devastation I was enduring. I wondered whether I could ever feel at peace again, but I so wanted the hurt to go away. I prayed for the anger and unforgiveness at my then husband to minimize, because it was consuming my mind and draining me emotionally.

The magnitude of problems I was facing as a result of suddenly being thrust into the world of being a single mom and woman who had no full-time employment but a big heaping of full-time financial obligations is impossible to even explain. Every problem felt too big to handle, and I felt less and less capable of surviving with each passing day. I stopped sleeping, lost weight due to a loss of appetite, and even my hair began to thin out dramatically. Again, I knew stress was silently killing me from the inside out.

The day came when I couldn't take anymore. I ached for that peace I had discovered years ago, but lost, to find its way back into my heart. So instead of praying for God to fix all my problems, I prayed for him to fix me. I needed God to heal the broken pieces of my heart, weaving a soft thread of his scarlet peace through the frayed edges of my life. I got on my knees—or, should I say, fell to my knees—and surrendered my problems, my stressors, my worries, and my fears over to God. I promised to trust him with my present and my future going forward, and admitted to the realization that my attempts at trying to handle it all and letting stress run my life were clearly not working. I gave up and gave in to God.

It didn't happen instantaneously, but I could sense a change happening over time. I began to feel a sense of peace and serenity I could not explain, even though all my problems were still there to greet me each morning when I woke up. One day, I found myself whistling as I cleaned the kitchen after dinner, and I suddenly realized I had gone hours without focusing on all the issues that plagued my life and the brokenness of my heart. As a result, without even really being aware, I felt joyful and free, despite the less-than-joyful circumstance I was going through.

I remember thinking to myself, *How could this be? How can I feel joyful when life is still such a disaster? How could I feel full of peace, even if momentarily, when I'm living in the wake of the destruction of a failed marriage?*

For a moment I felt confused, wondering, *Why am I so calm? Why have I not been obsessing about all my problems every second today? Why am I not more distraught and worried, like normal? Why do I not feel that burning anger in my heart anymore? How is it possible that I am feeling happy in the middle of this terrible storm in my life?* It had caught me off guard, and the more I pondered it, it surpassed my understanding.

Then God quickened my heart and reminded me that just a few days earlier I had turned that problem over to him. I had asked him to intervene and to fill me with a peace that surpassed my understanding. I had begged for joy amid this joyless time. I had asked, and he had given.

God heard that prayer of anxiousness and desperation. He heard my loud pleading for peace, and he answered. He had dried my tears and lifted that weight off my shoulders. He was now carrying my cross, and I no longer had to. I had sought out a cure from the Great Physician, and he had provided it. Not a cure for the problem but a cure for my heart as I lived with the problem in his strength, and under the refuge of his love.

I want the same for you. I want you to discover that amazing feeling of hope and freedom that can be achieved once you realize the toxic disease of stress is not normal and definitely not worth the costs. Just because everyone is living in a frazzled state of mind doesn't mean you have to. The world doesn't have to have power over your inner peace. It is possible to have a peace that surpasses your understanding, regardless of what is going on in your life, as promised in Philippians 4:7: "Then you will experience God's peace, which exceeds anything we can understand. His peace will guard your hearts and minds as you live in Christ Jesus."

Christ is waiting patiently for you to call out to him so he can pour his peace into your life. My heart longs for Christ to use this book to lead you into a place of serenity that can only be found through a relationship with him and through trusting that peace is possible, even when your circumstances threaten to make you believe otherwise.

We need his strength, guidance, peace, and joy more than we will ever know; and the longer we continue to ignore the problem, the more destruction this silent killer will cause. Unfortunately, millions of people will keep on doing what they have always done, even if it's detrimental to their health and their future, simply because everybody else is doing it and because society has accepted stress as the norm and adapted to it. Even though swimming against the current takes more effort and dedication than following the crowd, it will always pay off in the long run.

Swimming against the Current in Parenting

Parenting and child rearing are among the top five stressors of the general population, and I can understand why. My children are all in their twenties now, but I vividly remember those days when I felt like the stress of being a parent just might be the death of me, and

I recall all those other days when I absolutely couldn't get enough of my sweet children. But despite my larger-than-life love for them, sometimes parental exhaustion would hit hard.

When children are little, the demands they place on a parent are physically exhausting, to say the least. But as they grow into adolescence, the physical exhaustion is quickly replaced by emotional exhaustion in its highest form.

Instead of our bodies suffering through sleepless nights and the constant smell of poopy diapers, our hearts suffer with worry over whether our children will make it home safely and whether they are strong enough to stand up for what is right in the face of peer pressure. In fact, despite all my stressful experiences in life, I honestly don't think I knew what real stress was until I was faced with the daunting task of raising teenagers.

Trying to raise up godly children in an ungodly world can be draining. There is so much stuff to deal with every day that we pour ourselves out and sometimes end up feeling empty and discouraged.

During those trying years of raising adolescents, there was one phrase that would make my head spin like something in a horror movie. One phrase that when it slipped over the lips of my children's mouths, their eyes would widen with immediate regret and they would wish they could suck the words back in. The words "But everybody else . . ." Them's are fighting words, which always held the ammunition to invoke a serious mommy meltdown.

Maybe you can relate, because you too have had your fill of the "everybody else" card being dealt. In fact, you may even feel like you are swimming upstream against a rapid, powerful current of hands-off parenting that seems to be a growing trend in our society. It is easy to see why that style of parenting is becoming so popular—it appears less stressful.

After all, who doesn't want less stress? Who wouldn't rather avoid engaging in hostile arguments, enforcing curfews, implementing discipline, and doling out punishments? Who wouldn't want to quit the full-time job of monitoring whereabouts, tracking activity, and approving outfit and friend choices? The temptation for parents to go along with what "everybody else" is doing, especially if it means keeping some shred of peace in the household, is sometimes stronger than the strength to persevere through the most stressful parenting years. However, the one thing that sets Christian parents apart from the rest of the world is the willingness to faithfully persevere in their parenting values, no matter how stressful the journey becomes, and no matter how unpopular it makes them.

Christian parents are called to be in the world but not of the world and to be set apart for their children's sake—not set aside by their children when they reach the age of fourteen. Instead of allowing the stress of parenting to tempt us to throw in the towel, we need to throw ourselves on our knees every day, praying for their safety and their decision-making and asking God to get a good, strong grasp on their hearts before something or someone else does.

Proverbs 22:6, a popular verse on the topic of parenting, says, "Train a child in the way he should go, and when he is old he will not turn from it" (NIV). Training a child up in the way he or she should go does not stop when we leave the sanctuary. It is a call to pursue God's ways every day with unwavering determination and unending perseverance and to learn to manage the never-ending onslaught of "stuff" without giving up. There will always be cases when even the best efforts to raise a child with a solid foundation of faith may seem futile when that child appears to be rejecting God's teaching or choosing paths that are not good for them. However, as a parent, I am encouraged by the words found in James 1:12: "Blessed is the man who perseveres under trial, because when he has stood the test, he will receive the crown of life that God has promised to those who love him" (NIV).

So who will be blessed? Those who persevere. The stress of parenting is very real but *well* worth it in the long run.

In this verse, although it was not specifically written with reference to parenting, James encourages us to not give in to temptation—not only temptations to sin but any temptations that go against what glorifies God. When I thought about temptations from a parenting perspective, several things came to mind: The temptation not to worry about what my kids watch on television because the world is saturated with bad language, sexual images, and violence everywhere anyway. The temptation to overlook dishonesty rather than taking time to discuss the importance of character and integrity and to implement discipline as needed. The temptation to allow my teenagers to go wherever they want to go just so I won't be the "mean mom" who always says no. The temptation to avoid deep conversations about drugs, alcohol, and sexual purity because they are not fun subjects to talk about.

The temptation to hold onto disappointment, hurt, or resentment when my children make mistakes, instead of forgiving and loving unconditionally. The temptation to lose my temper rather than practice self-control and patience. The temptation to let the church teach my children about God instead of making faith and prayer a priority in our home.

As we persevere through all the stress that comes along with raising children, we can have hope in knowing that God is always working behind the scenes in our children's lives, while we are planting seeds for fruit in their hearts along the way. But seed planting requires great perseverance. I vividly remember one particularly stressful day years ago when my daughters were in high school. They were both in their rooms, where I had sent them to calm their emotions down while I was feeling overwhelmed with my own and dealing with a stress and frustration level that was off the chart. So I did the only thing I could think of to do—I retreated to my front porch to be alone and to pray.

It had been yet another dramatic day in a household with maturing teenage girls. One was upset because she was not allowed to attend a social outing that "everybody else" was going to but that I just didn't have a good feeling about. The other was upset because of a recent breakup with a boyfriend and had become more emotional when I tried to console her with what I thought was loving motherly advice.

Leading up to this stressful day, we had spent weeks dealing with a couple of very mean girl bullies at school who had made it their personal life goal to start hurtful rumors and cause heartache to innocent girls, one of whom was my daughter. My anger at these individuals, my heartache for my daughter, and my frustration with how the school system was handling the issue (or not handling it, I should say) had turned my nerves into a knotted mass. Not to mention the ongoing friend/ex-friend issues, fitting in, self-esteem, fashion woes, cheerleading drama, daily sports practices, and peer pressure situations that bobbed in and out of our lives every day like small ships tossed in stormy seas. And that's just the tip of the stress iceberg we were all living on.

The stress of parenting had seriously worn me down. I longed for some peace and quiet; and although I would have loved to escape my problems by hopping on a plane to a Caribbean beach for the day, I knew what I really needed was to be alone with my feelings and with God. So, on the front porch I sat, soaking in the sunshine and secretly longing for the days gone by when things seemed so much easier and less stressful, to say the least. As I breathed in the aroma of the spring air, watching the bumblebees drawing nectar from the flowers and listening to the birds sweetly chirping, my eyes fell upon a piece of the past. Tucked shallowly in the pine straw beside the front porch steps, under the shadow of a huge holly tree, were two faded, slightly cracked, plastic Easter eggs.

My thoughts were instantly jerked back to many years ago when my daughters were small. My mind played out a memory as if it were happening right in front of my eyes. I watched two dainty, blonde-headed, blue-eyed little beauties frolicking in the thick, green grass, wearing frilly white and pink Easter dresses, holding hands as they skipped. I could see their little fingers wrapped tightly around their wicker Easter baskets as they excitedly hid brightly colored Easter eggs around the yard and under the holly bushes—bushes that were then twelve inches tall but now stood at twelve feet.

To my own surprise, tears began trickling down my face. Things seemed so easy when my little girls thought I was the most wonderful person in the universe, and the hardest question of the day was whether they could have a snack before dinner. But as I grappled with my emotions, I began to wonder if all the stress of parenting was even worth it. If trying to stand firm in my commitment to raise my children in the ways of the Lord—even if they didn't like it and even if other parents thought I was an over-protective Jesus freak—would ever pay off.

God is always faithful, and in this moment of self-doubt, he knew the reassurance I needed to hear. I sensed his whisper through the soft breeze that tousled my hair, reminding me that he had called me to be more than a mommy. He called me to be a mom who raises her children according to his Word, even when it's not easy. A mom who perseveres through the stress because of her commitment to raising children who know the Lord. A mom who sticks to her convictions, even when it would be easier and much less stressful to give in and just let them do what "everybody else" is doing. A mom who sleeps soundly at night, knowing she made good decisions for the well-being of her children, even if those children go to bed mad at her. As I thought about all these things, reminiscing on the past and breathing in the present, my two precious teenage daughters discovered my hidden whereabouts on the porch. As we all three sat on the steps together, Kaitlyn ironically pointed out the eggs under the tree and my tears flowed again. Both of my girls looked at each other with perplexed expressions and then looked at me as if I had sprouted horns. *Why was Mom crying over an old, faded Easter egg?*

Then we all started laughing, shared some much-needed hugs, and spent the next half hour talking openly about feelings, life, and outfits for the next day. I suddenly felt a feeling of peace wash over me, knowing that God had given me a glimpse of the past and this sweet moment with my daughters to reenergize my spirit and equip me to embrace today and tomorrow with confidence as I persisted in my quest to be the mom he called me to be. Although I know I am an imperfect mom raising imperfect kids, I believe God calls us to love our children enough to sometimes swim against the current.

Those faded Easter eggs were a symbol of what life once was but a sweet reminder that even though the seasons of life may change, God never does. He is always there to help us stand strong and bring us peace in the midst of stressful seasons of life when we need it most in our parenting journey, whether we are enduring sleepless nights and changing poopy diapers or enforcing curfews and molding hearts.

Parenting is stressful—in more ways than one—but through our perseverance and commitment to staying strong in our beliefs, despite whether everyone else is, we will be able to experience the joy discussed in 3 John 1:4, which says, "I have no greater joy than to hear that my children are walking in the truth" (NIV).

If you are suffering with parental exhaustion and stress, you are not alone. But if you are wondering if you can survive another stressful day, maybe it's time you enjoy a little sabbatical on your front porch and ask God for perseverance to be the mom, or dad, God called you to be.

In the same way, the journey to becoming less stressed in a busy, chaotic, stress-driven culture is equally as difficult as being a Christian parent. Trying to swim against the current norm of society and learn to depend on Jesus for peace instead of the ways of the world is even harder.

In either circumstance, Jesus holds the peace we long for. And even if nobody else is looking for it and everybody else is going with the flow, we will always know where real peace can be found.

⟋ Reflection Questions

1. What practical stress relief methods have you tried? How did these make you feel?

2. Have the worldly stress-relief tactics that you have tried provided any stress relief at all? If so, was that relief temporary and superficial, or permanent and life changing?

3. What unhealthy habits or possibly harmful methods of coping with your stress have you developed over time?

4. What healthy changes can you begin making today to better cope with your stress? Ask God for the wisdom and strength to overcome unhealthy habits and begin forming new habits that will result in positive change. Write out your prayerful thoughts here.

5. Do you believe that the key to managing your stress, and regaining your peace and joy, begins with Christ? Set aside some time to focus on God's promises about peace. Consider looking up these verses and ask God to speak to your heart through them: Psalm 16:8, Psalm 18:1–2, Psalm 18:6, 2 Samuel 22:7, Matthew 11:28–30, 2 Corinthians 4:16–18, Ecclesiastes 7:14, and Psalm 46:1.

6. Are you possibly suffering from a case of parental exhaustion? If so, invite God into the picture, and ask him for peace in the midst of your stressful parenting "stuff."

7. Have you been tempted to take a back seat in your teenager's life, simply because it seems like it would be less stressful? If your answer is yes, consider making a list of the pros and cons of taking a back seat, and ask God to help you see why sometimes the toughest road is the one that leads to the greatest blessings.

If you have allowed the frustration and stress of parenting to keep you from being the parent you feel called to be, ask God to give you clarity about changes you can make to get back on track, the spiritual courage to stand firm in your Christian parenting beliefs even when it's hard, and the emotional strength to persevere.

Stress-Busting Scriptures

The Lord is a refuge for the oppressed, a stronghold in times of trouble. Those who know your name will trust in you, for you, Lord, have never forsaken those who seek you.

Psalm 9:9–10 NIV

You are my hiding place; you will protect me from trouble and surround me with songs of deliverance. I will instruct you and teach you in the way you should go; I will counsel you and watch over you.

Psalm 32:7–8 NIV

This is what the Sovereign Lord, the Holy One of Israel, says: "In repentance and rest is your salvation, in quietness and trust is your strength, but you would have none of it."

Isaiah 30:15 NIV

"For I know the plans I have for you," says the Lord. "They are plans for good and not for disaster, to give you a future and a hope."

Jeremiah 29:11

Rejoice in our confident hope. Be patient in trouble, and keep on praying.

Romans 12:12

CHAPTER FOUR

Time for Change

Just before quitting my job many years ago, I was already at the breaking point when the final blow was inflicted. The hit was hard—my boss informed me I would soon be required to work more hours in the office—it pushed me over the edge toward serious life change. Since my employment there had already reached an unbearable stage, evidenced by daily bouts of nausea and tears shed on the way to work every morning, this news felt like a stake in my heart. I finally had to accept the reality that this place was not where God wanted me to be. So, after much discussion and prayer, my then husband and I agreed it would be in my best interest (and that of my family, my sanity, and my stress level) to take a leap of faith and resign.

As strange as it may sound, the idea of giving up my career and my income caused me even more anxiety than I was already experiencing, despite knowing that stress and misery had become the heartbeat of my daily existence—although I was still unaware my health problems were resulting from the level of duress I endured at work. So, after weeks of inner turmoil, I reluctantly decided to resign.

Even though I was very uncomfortable in this job, the thought of being unemployed was even more uncomfortable. I had been employed since graduating from college. I had always been a "working mom." I thought my job was my identity, as if it was what gave me value in this world. I had not yet discovered that my true value and worth came from Christ alone, not from my name on a paycheck. And I certainly did not know this drastic, sacrificial change God had called me to make would help me discover the new me, much less that it was actually going to save my life. He had waited years for me to obey, and I finally surrendered, but with a somewhat grumpy attitude, I must confess.

You see, I had felt God's call on my heart five years earlier to leave my job and focus on serving in ministry but had pushed the idea aside as ludicrous and absurd. How could I quit work when we have bills to pay? How could I leave when I've been working so long to climb the corporate ladder? But God had been trying to get my attention, and finally, when I was at my lowest state (physically and emotionally), I was not only ready to listen but ready to obey. I figured nothing could be worse than the stress-consumed existence I was already enduring.

With mixed emotions, I pushed past my fear and doubts and finally turned in my resignation. With each passing day of my six-week resignation period, God gently drew me closer and closer, reassuring me his plans were better than mine, even though I could not understand them yet, and encouraging me to trust him. He poured people into my path to encourage me in my choices—people I had worked with for years whom I never even knew were believers.

God knew a positive change in my life was long overdue, and I finally came to a place in my heart and mind where I agreed. I was finally *ready* to be set free from the prison of stress I had been living in and embrace whatever plans he had for me with open arms.

When Change Seems Strange

The first couple of months of being voluntarily unemployed were, shall I say, very strange. I felt as if I didn't know who I was. I hardly knew what to do with myself. I would wake up in the morning and scurry around to get the children ready for school, but once they were gone I was like a little puppy lost in a field of hundreds of acres.

I felt disconnected from what used to be my life, from people, from business meetings, from goals, and from adult interaction. I could not get my head out of the game. I spoke with someone from my old office every day just to see what was going on, who was doing what, how the search was going for my replacement, and what office politics were still running rampant. I was sure I still needed to be plugged in to find any self-worth at all.

But then the strangeness of change began to feel less strange, and I began to experience some refreshing changes. A few months after resigning, I began to see the little glimmer of light God had been waving in front of my eyes all along, like the beam from a lighthouse far off in the distance that was getting closer and brighter. As I adjusted to my new lifestyle at home, away from my leather chair, high-rise office, oh-so-important responsibilities, and overwhelming office issues, my stress slowly began to dissipate.

I gradually grew to love being at home, basking in my newfound freedom to be who I wanted to be, and not who a corporation expected me to be. I enjoyed not having to constantly defend and justify my abilities and my character. I also realized the damage that had been done to my self-esteem as a result of working for someone who treated me as an inferior human being. Needless to say, I loved the fact that I could now look to my new Boss for confirmation of my worth—Jesus himself. And this Boss adored me so much he had given his life for me.

After that period of adjustment, I began to realize I had been on a corporate train wreck for years while never recognizing the emotional prison I had been willingly trapped in. Stress and chaos used to be my normal, but now God was blessing me with the new normal that he knew was best all along. Peace. Not a lack of problems or issues (remember I'm still a parent of teens at this point and experiencing marital struggles) but a peace only God could provide.

My excitement grew about embracing the life that God had in store for me. As my faith blossomed and I devoted more time to my relationship with Christ and serving in ministry, he lovingly proceeded to give me tiny glimpses of the wonderful plans he had for me, just as he promised in Jeremiah 29:11 when he said, "For I know the plans I have for you. . . . They are plans for good and not for disaster, to give you a future and a hope."

I began taking little steps of faith to do what I knew God had called me to do years earlier. I devoted many hours trying to learn how to be a Christian speaker and writer and how to get that goal off the ground. Now that I was seeking God's guidance instead of following my own agenda for worldly success, I was able to dedicate my time and energies to the things that really mattered.

Over time, I slowly began to see some other strange changes. Not just in my stress level, my faith walk, and my overall emotional health, but in my physical health as well. At first it seemed peculiar, and it took me a few months to figure out what was going on. Then one day, out of the blue, I noticed something absolutely amazing—I had risen from my bed after a good night's sleep and felt a strange sensation, a new zest and energy for the day that I hadn't felt in a very long time. I was ready to get up and get moving and felt enthusiastic about the things I planned to do that day. Then it hit me. That strange feeling I was experiencing? I simply felt good.

In fact, I felt great! What in the world was this strange phenomenon of feeling good, healthy, and happy?!

I suddenly thought about those health issues and all the doctor's appointments I had been to, relentlessly trying to find a diagnosis for every ailment. It dawned on me it had been weeks since I even thought about whether I was going to live to a ripe old age. Then, as if a light bulb switched on in my mind, I became acutely aware I was miraculously less stressed and it felt incredible! It had been so long since I had been less stressed, I had forgotten how it felt to be happy and at peace. And trust me, friends, it was a good, good feeling that came solely because of the powerful presence of God in my life and the fact that I was now walking in obedience to his will, instead of my own.

If you glean only one point of wisdom from this entire book, let it be this: less stress does not come from removing yourself from a stressful job. You truly become less stressed when you discover the God of peace and walk in obedience with what he has called you to do. Real peace comes when you make God the center of your life, instead of the last resort. My stress lessened when I learned to turn to him for stress relief, instead of the ways of society. Most importantly, stress relief became a reality when two little words crossed my lips . . . *Yes, Lord*. God had waited years to hear me utter those words, and I can't help but assume my life would have been much less stressed all along if only I had listened and surrendered to his ways sooner.

But leaving that job and watching my health return was a huge eye-opener, and for the first time ever, I was able to see with great clarity the poison stress really is and the damage it can inflict on our physical bodies.

Called to Change

Several years before all this stress erupted at work like a volcano with a vengeance, God had placed a call upon my life, which I had blatantly and consciously ignored. Let's backtrack for a moment and delve into the details of where my journey first began.

It all started one beautiful spring day when I found myself at a women's ministry seminar at my church. Although I was attending church regularly at the time, I was more of a pew dweller than an active Christian. I had never participated in a women's church function before. But for reasons I didn't know at the time (which in hindsight could only have been the nudging of the Holy Spirit), I felt a desire to go to this seminar. I had every intention of enjoying a Saturday morning to myself, free from crying little ones and dirty laundry. I planned on singing some praise and worship songs, listening to a typical message of encouragement, eating refreshments, and sharing a few laughs with friends. I certainly did not expect anything out of the ordinary to occur, but God had something extraordinary planned.

As I sat there in the sanctuary, listening to the speaker share her powerful, life-changing testimony, I felt the presence of God stronger than ever before. At the time, it was a new feeling for me, and I couldn't quite understand what I was experiencing. I had heard people talk about feeling the presence of the Holy Spirit but had never experienced it for myself so I had decided that type of thing only happened to holy rollers—which I certainly was not.

Despite my skepticism, I knew what I was feeling had to be God. It was heavy, yet light. Suffocating, yet freeing. Nerve-racking, yet peaceful. I felt as if I could reach out and touch him right then and there. You see, when I walked into that sanctuary wearing a big smile on my face, I was hiding a heart that was shattered. I had spent years feeling worthless—like a broken, throwaway person because of the sins in my past. I felt devoid of any value. Unredeemable. Unlovable. Unforgivable. Despicable in God's eyes. Upon hearing the speaker's testimony, which was astonishingly similar to my own—the deep, raw wounds in my heart became exposed. The windows of my soul were flung wide open, and God could reach down to even the darkest parts. I was sobbing and praying for God to forgive me for past sins—sins that had held me captive in guilt and shame for years, sins that had kept my stress level at an all-time high as I harbored them in my heart and ensnared them with my own insecurities, sins that had caused me to believe the lies of the enemy. The enemy who had convinced me day after day that God could never forgive someone like me, much less love me or have a purpose for me. As I begged for God's forgiveness once again, I felt his mercy and compassion flooding over me like surging waters.

In this sweet, powerful moment with God, while my requests for his love and forgiveness still hung in the air, I felt his power wash through my soul and the weight of my sin being lifted away. I could feel the difference in my heart, and my spiritual ears were awakened for the very first time. Instantly, I was overcome with praise, gratitude, and awe. I wanted to stand up and shout out to the heavens with open arms, publicly expressing my thankfulness and reverence. But for fear of what others might think of me, I stayed motionless and paralyzed in my pew.

As I relished in the freedom that I had just received, my heart ached to hear a divine message reassuring me that the feelings I was experiencing were real. As I sat there in the pew, eyes closed, spiritual ears open, hot tears stinging my face and bursting forth like water from a dam that had just given way to the pressure—it happened.

Suddenly, the Lord's voice echoed so loudly that it startled me. My eyes thrust open and I glanced around to see if anyone else had heard it. Since I saw no commotion in the sanctuary, and no other women appearing to be confused, alarmed, or frantically gazing upward with a look of *Who said that!?* on their faces, I determined that I was, indeed, the only one who had heard his voice. It was a divine message, meant for me alone.

I was actually stunned to think God had spoken to little ol' me. I thought that only happened in books or movies, not in real life. I thought that only happened to people who were thoroughly spiritual and righteous—not pathetic sinners like me. The sheer thought that God had paused in his job of running the universe to lean down and speak peace, truth, and purpose into a broken-hearted, stressed-out young woman's heart stopped me in my tracks.

He had spoken, and I had heard. He was loud, yet he was silent. Gently but firmly, God spoke four little words that would forever alter the course of my life. He simply said, "*Tracie, go . . . and share.*" As I sat there stunned, my mind raced with thoughts not only because I had heard God's audible voice in my spirit but because I was confused . . . *Go where? And share what?* His answers to my questions were much more subtle but just as clear.

The realization of what he was calling me to do left me speechless. You see, he was calling me to go to a new place and to trust him to lead the way. He was calling me to quit my job—a job that was causing me too much stress anyway but that I had never contemplated leaving. He was calling me to share the painful memories of my past with other women who needed to hear a message of hope and forgiveness. He was calling me to help other women discover the transforming peace that I had just received. But instead of allowing my thankfulness for who he was to fuel me with courage and passion, I was overcome with a sudden sensation of debilitating fear when I considered what "going" and "sharing" really meant. So, as my fears overshadowed my gratitude, I quickly and adamantly answered God's call by saying, "*No.*" There was absolutely no way I could ever have the courage to do that—not even twenty seconds' worth.

As honored and humbled as I was to have experienced such a divine God encounter, I had never intended for my life to be interrupted that day. I simply had no interest in carrying out the plan for my life that God had just laid out in my heart. I had a career to consider and a salary that I depended on. So what if I was stressed? Did it really matter? Just the thought of following his call made me feel weak in the knees. The idea of being transparent and vulnerable—open to judgment and criticism, becoming the brunt of jokes, being the subject of whispers of gossip, talking in front of groups of people—made me feel physically ill.

Although I walked out of the sanctuary that morning a transformed woman on the inside, I was too terrified to obey his call on the outside. I turned my back on his plan and began walking down the winding road of life that I thought seemed like the better choice. A life that would be so consumed with twists and turns and overwhelming stress that it would leave my head spinning.

I chose a life of stress instead of the sweet life God had designed for me for two reasons. The first reason was that I had failed to ever build a strong relationship with Christ. Although I had spoken the words to accept Jesus Christ as my Savior as a child, I was more of a churchgoer than a true Christ "follower." I had spent years going through the motions of Christianity, oblivious to the fact that I had a religion, not a relationship. The second reason was that I was just too afraid to trust God with my life—a sure sign of a lack of relationship with Christ. I was unsure if he was really capable of providing and protecting or if he really had a plan for a broken woman like me. My feelings of unworthiness compounded my fears, and, as a result, I did not know how to trust God, and I certainly didn't know he was the answer to my stress.

If I had only known how beautiful and peace-filled God's path would be or had possessed the faith to honestly believe his plan was better than mine. But, as a result of the lack of an intimate relationship with Christ, I spent the next five years running as far in the other direction as I could from his plan. I ran back into my high-rise building, back to following a career dream that God never intended for me in the first place, and back to thinking that happiness would come with a big salary and a big corporate agenda. All of the adversity and stress that I encountered during those five years of disobedience are what you read about in the previous chapters. All those years I spent drowning in stress and health problems could have been prevented if only I had said, *"Yes, Lord"* much sooner. His peace had been available to me throughout my whole ordeal, but it took me letting go of the rope and plunging into the pit of toxic stress before I decided that maybe, just maybe, his ways were better.

As I look back on my life now, it is so obvious my stress came not only from the external pressures of my job, the hurtful people in my life, or the difficult adversities that I faced, but also from the internal stress of not following God's call on my life. Stress was a by-product of not knowing God personally, not trusting him with my whole heart, and seeking peace and purpose from the world instead of from him.

God does not call each of his children to leave their careers behind as he did me, but he definitely has a uniquely designed plan for each one. He calls each of us to serve him in the unique way, and in the unique places, he has equipped us to glorify him in.

Many of you reading this book have wonderful careers and feel confident you are exactly where God has called you to be. I pray God is blessing your hard work and commitment and you feel his affirmation in what you are doing while shining his light through you on the people he has put in your path. But I also pray you stay aware of your stress levels and don't let them steal the best of you or your life.

Regardless of whether you work in a corporate high-rise or a home office, as a stay-at-home mom or dad, in a warehouse, at the mall, in ministry, on the mission field, or on staff at a church—if you are in God's unique and destined will for your life and are making your relationship with him a priority, you can keep stress at bay because real peace will take up residence in your heart.

◯ᴧ Reflection Questions

1. What changes could you make in your life that might eliminate stress? List them here.

2. Regarding the changes you just listed, what obstacles might stand in the way? How can you proactively prepare to overcome those obstacles?

3. Are your secret fears, insecurities, or past sins preventing you from making necessary changes that would help alleviate some of your stressors? What can you do to start trusting God with your whole heart and with your whole life and start accepting how valuable you are to him?

4. What steps can you take today to begin tackling your fears and moving forward in faith? Consider these verses when answering that question: 1 Chronicles 28:20, Psalm 27:1, Psalm 56:3–4, Isaiah 41:13, Isaiah 54:4, 2 Timothy 1:7, Hebrews 13:5–6.

5. Have you ever wondered if there is more to life than what you are currently doing? Is it possible you have been too stressed and distracted to consider that God might have a better plan for you? If so, take a moment to jot down any God-sized dreams that have been hidden in your heart, no matter how impossible or far-fetched they may seem. Pray for God to make it clear what your next steps should be, remembering that God only asks that we take one step at a time, trusting him along the way.

*Faith is taking the first step even when
you don't see the whole staircase.*

Martin Luther King Jr.

6. Have you ever knowingly told God "no"? Write about something you need to say, "Yes, Lord" to.

7. Has God ever prompted you to make a change in your life, and when you obeyed, you could see that his ways were best? Write down those spiritual markers in your life and spend time thanking God for using all things to his glory. Let them serve as encouragement for trusting God with your future.

Stress-Busting Scriptures

Don't copy the behavior and customs of this world,
but let God transform you into a new person by changing the way
you think. Then you will learn to know God's will for you,
which is good and pleasing and perfect.

Romans 12:2

Then [Jesus] said, "I tell you the truth,
unless you turn from your sins and become like little children, you
will never get into the Kingdom of Heaven."

Matthew 18:3

That is why the LORD says, "Turn to me now, while there is time.
Give me your hearts. Come with fasting, weeping, and mourning.
Don't tear your clothing in your grief, but tear you hears instead."
Return to the LORD your God, for he is merciful and compassionate,
slow to get angry and filled with unfailing love.
He is eager to relent and not punish.

Joel 2:12–13

It is better to take refuge in the LORD than to trust in people.

Psalm 118:8

O LORD, I give my life to you. I trust in you, my God!
Do not let me be disgraced, or let my enemies rejoice in my defeat.

Psalm 25:1–2

CHAPTER FIVE

Take Back Your Life

Have you ever wondered who you really are, or where the person went that you used to be? Have you ever dreamed about the person you wanted to be but felt unable to become that person because of circumstances in your life, pressures on your heart, sins of your past, or the weight of daily chaos? Do you wish you could relax in a beach chair and spend a few hours submerging your feet in the gentle waves lapping on the shore, but you are stretched too thin to even consider a moment's rest? Maybe you have vague recollections of a time when you were footloose and fancy-free, lying in soft grass on a beautiful spring day and watching the clouds go by as you tried to figure out which ones looked like recognizable shapes. Or maybe you love to reminisce about distant childhood memories of swinging on a rope swing in your grandmother's backyard, picking up pecans from the pecan trees, and frolicking around in the sprinkler in the hot sun. A smile may come to your face as you think back to the awesome sense of freedom surging through your spirit as you rode your bicycle through your neighborhood or played hide-and-seek with your friends until you heard your mom calling you home for dinner.

Ahhhh, those were the days. If you had a relatively normal childhood, you may remember those simple, carefree days too. The days when we were young, with no jobs or financial worries, and our only concerns were whether or not we were going to be invited to the popular kid's birthday party.

I like to imagine what it would be like to go back to those laid-back and worry-free days. I remember the days when I watched my teenage daughters scurrying through life, and feeling a little twinge of secret envy. They were so full of energy and always filled with excitement about what each new day would bring, no matter how small or insignificant. They would spend their time counting down the weeks until summer vacation, hanging out with their friends, and making plans for college careers, while their whole future seemed like an exciting blank canvas just waiting to be painted. It's funny how when we are young, we never envision ourselves living a life bogged down with chaos and stress, void of adventure and excitement. But unfortunately, as we grow up, our stress can begin to grow at an even faster rate than our bodies do, threatening to steal our joy and peace, especially if we lose sight of our sense of innocent enthusiasm and our childlike faith.

On the other hand, maybe your childhood isn't something you want to reminisce about at all. Maybe you struggle to remember any times of peace in days gone by. Maybe you suffered from physical or sexual abuse as a child, mental and emotional abuse, or neglect and a lack of feeling loved or accepted. Maybe you had an abortion as a young woman and have never been able to shake the shame or remorse. Maybe your family struggled financially, or divorce wreaked havoc on your home.

Maybe you feel as if the pain in your heart that has evolved over a lifetime of hard experiences prevents you from even being able to fathom having a life of peace, much less a heart full of joy.

Perhaps you feel like you would never in a million years want to relive your childhood, because it was more stressful than your life today. Could those memories of difficult times possibly be adding to your current stress, even if you think you have dealt with those emotional scars?

Whether our childhood was peaceful, chaotic, or painful, it doesn't have to dictate how we live our lives today. We can believe that a life of peace and less stress is feasible if we rely on our God, who promises it can be.

Mark 10:27 says, "Jesus looked at them intently and said, 'Humanly speaking, it is impossible. But not with God. Everything is possible with God.'" Living a life full of joy and void of chronic stress may seem impossible to you today as you find yourself pondering all the difficult situations in your life—the hardships you have endured, the pain you have experienced, the struggles you are currently facing, or the looming hopelessness of the future. But true joy and peace are within your reach if you are reaching out to the right place for help—Jesus Christ. Peace is not a matter of life or circumstances; it's a matter of the heart.

God could change our circumstances at any time, if he chose to do so, but he is always more interested in changing us *through* our circumstances than changing our circumstances themselves. Everything is possible with God, because he said so.

When God Seems Absent

There are countless stories in the Bible of people who faced great adversity and stress but who persevered in Christ, finding peace and blessing as a result. One of those people can be found in the book of 1 Samuel, and her name was Hannah.

When we are introduced to Hannah, we find out she was one of Elkanah's two wives; the other wife was Peninnah. Even though having more than one wife was a common practice in biblical times, Hannah's stress probably began at the onset of having to share her husband with another woman. I simply cannot imagine how emotionally challenging that must have been.

Though an accepted practice in biblical times, polygamy was never God's intention for marriage when he instituted it in the Garden of Eden. Women were not meant to have to share husbands, and God did not create them to be robots with no emotions. Marriage was created to be a loving, monogamous union between one man and one woman, where adultery was forbidden and divorce was not an option.

This society that condoned polygamy was part of the culture Hannah lived in and obviously caused her tumultuous stress and heartache. However, the real stressor for Hannah is revealed in 1 Samuel 1:2 when we read that while her cowife, Peninnah, had children, Hannah's struggle with infertility left her childless. According to 1 Samuel 1:3, it is implied her infertility had been going on for years, leaving Hannah in daily anguish. It also says each year, Elkanah, along with Hannah and Peninnah with all her kids in tow, would travel to Shiloh to worship and offer sacrifices. This is where Hannah's heartache would be personified in its highest form.

You see, each year when they would travel to Shiloh, and probably on a day-in and day-out basis, Peninnah would torment Hannah with words of ridicule. 1 Samuel 1:6-7 says, "So Peninnah would taunt Hannah and make fun of her because the LORD had kept her from having children. Year after year it was the same—Peninnah would taunt Hannah as they went to the Tabernacle. Each time, Hannah would be reduced to tears and would not even eat."

Hannah was tormented, not only because of the stigma and shame of being barren and the emptiness in her heart caused by her lack of children, but also because of the great persecution that was mercilessly bestowed upon her by Peninnah. After years of anguish, the day finally came when Hannah reached her breaking point. Even when Elkanah saw her crying and refusing to eat and reminded her how happy she should be because he was devoted to her and her needs (verse 8), she absolutely could not contain her overwhelming sorrow anymore.

She had had quite enough of Peninnah and her self-centered, inconsiderate, hurtful ways. She was tired of the emotional abuse and endless ridicule that Peninnah inflicted upon her. She was fed up with always being treated as an inferior woman due to circumstances beyond her control. She was tired of feeling ashamed, broken, empty-hearted, and empty-handed.

Her emotions must have surely ravaged her heart to the core. I can only assume she tried to be happy in knowing Elkanah loved and adored her. I bet she tried to stay focused on her blessings rather than being consumed with yearning for the blessings she had yet to receive. I can also imagine how helpless she must have felt to remedy this problem. All of these things combined most likely ushered her into a deep pit of hopelessness, where peace escaped her and stress filled every gaping crack in her heart. And I feel certain that when she was at her lowest point, Peninnah was there to continue with her emotional lashings.

We read in verses 6 and 7 Hannah had been going to the place of worship year after year, as was the custom, but this year, *something* was different. Hannah was stressed to the max. She was at the end of her rope. She desperately needed something to change.

She had been faithful and trusting of her Lord and had prayed for a child for years to no avail. She was in a place of complete dependence on God, because he was the only hope she had left. She wanted less stress and anxiety and more peace. She wanted less of her and more of God; and in her inconsolable despondency, she called out to him. She said, as noted in 1 Samuel 1:11, "O LORD Almighty, if you will only look upon your servant's misery and remember me" (NIV). Hannah was desperate to know that God saw her and her pain. She needed to be noticed. She wanted to be remembered. She longed to be touched by God, and she ached for a resolution to her stress.

Although Hannah had prayed about this problem before, probably hundreds of times, God had still not answered her prayers for a child. However, on this particular day, she was so desperate for God's intervention that she dropped to her knees and poured out her entire heart. She held nothing back and laid all her feelings and emotions at his feet. She was ready to take back her life, lay down her stress, and accept whatever plan God had for her. Peace at any cost.

She was so absolutely destitute and broken that she not only prayed but she prayed with fervency, gusto, and enthusiasm. She prayed out of her distress and great need with such passion and intensity that onlookers thought she was drunk. When Eli, the high priest, questioned her behavior, she answered in verses 15 and 16 by saying, "Oh no, sir! . . . I haven't been drinking wine or anything stronger. But I am very discouraged, and I was pouring out my heart to the LORD. Don't think I am a wicked woman! For I have been praying out of great anguish and sorrow." God then spoke through Eli, and he said to Hannah in verse 17, "Go in peace! May the God of Israel grant the request you have asked of him."

Hannah did have great faith, even though she felt weak at the time having endured so many years of adversity and torment from her cowife. But, when Hannah received a word of encouragement from Eli, she believed she had been given a message from God. Eli was a well-respected priest and judge, loved and admired by all who knew him. So when he spoke, people listened. She hung on his every word. In verse 18, Hannah responded to Eli by saying, "Oh, thank you, sir!" Then we are told "she went back and began to eat again, and she was no longer sad."

Why was she no longer sad? Why did she immediately regain her appetite? After all, she did not suddenly have a swollen, pregnant belly. Her circumstances were exactly the same. She was still a cowife of Elkanah, and she would still be traveling back home with that horrible Peninnah and all her kids.

So what was different? What had changed? The answer: Hannah's heart. Hannah had poured out her deepest hurts and longings to God and sincerely believed he had heard them after hearing Eli's words of comfort. She had no idea if, when, or how God would answer her prayers; but she believed whatever happened would be good—his good and pleasing will, despite what that may be. It seems she made a commitment to herself to be happy and cling to the peace only found through faith, especially in the face of great adversity that seems to have no end in sight.

You see, Hannah's faith was the answer to her stress. And, through that faith, she found peace, even though her life remained far from peaceful. Her struggle with infertility and tense relationship with cowife Peninnah remained the same, but her heart and mind did not. Her faith resulted in God working on her behalf. Hannah did not find peace because she left a stressful situation—she found peace because she had learned to depend on God's strength to rise above her stress.

This story has a happy ending in 1 Samuel 1:19–20 where we read, "The entire family got up early the next morning and went to worship the LORD once more. Then they returned home to Ramah. When Elkanah slept with Hannah, the LORD remembered her plea, and in due time she gave birth to a son. She named him Samuel, for she said, 'I asked the LORD for him.'"

I love that God gave Hannah a happy ending, and I believe our Heavenly Father wants us all to have happy endings, but we do live in a broken world where all of our dreams don't always come true. Even if God doesn't answer our prayers the way we had hoped, we can still rest in the peace he provides and learn to trust and believe his ways are always best.

A key point found in verse 19, crucial to our own faith walk and our quest for peace, is when we read that "the LORD remembered her." He remembered the faithful woman who had continued to love him and worship him despite her years of painful circumstances and heartache. He remembered the faithful woman who had sought his help and continued to persevere even when it appeared God wasn't listening. He remembered the woman who knew her only hope for a solution to her stress would be found in the One who had created her.

He remembered her, and despite all the emotional and physical suffering that she endured, she had remembered him. It was Hannah's strong faith that opened the door for the Lord to work in her life, and her faith led to peace and blessings.

The Lord could have given her a child at any time, even upon her first request spoken years earlier right after marrying Elkanah. Instead, he spent years grooming her heart, building her dependence and desperation for him, and preparing her for his plans. In this case, his plans were for her to give birth to a son whom she would fully dedicate to the Lord.

Because of her faith, Hannah became a different person, even when her circumstances stayed the same. God could have intervened in Hannah's circumstances at any time, but he chose to change Hannah's heart instead—the same way he often does in our lives, as well.

No matter what adversities we face or how difficult our circumstances are, God remembers us. Take comfort in knowing that God has not left you, even if it seems like he is absent in your life or that he does not see or care about what you are going through.

As we make our faith a priority and learn to trust in God's plans even if we do not understand them or like them, the doors will be slung wide open for God to enter our lives and begin his mighty work. During the wait, we are called to fall on our knees just like Hannah and pour out our hearts to him and surrender whatever it is standing in the way of living with peace in our hearts.

I have always heard that God is never late, he is seldom early, but he is always right on time. His timing is not our own. Hannah wanted a child for years, but God chose the perfect time, at his appointed moment, to bless her with one, in the scheme of his bigger picture. We may want many things that seem to be out of our reach, but trusting in God's timing gives us hope and strength to seek his peace during the wait.

But what should we do while we are waiting on God's perfect timing? What is our course of action after we place our circumstances into God's hands? The answer is not to sit idly by waiting on God to do something, but to actively strive for a change of heart, just like Hannah. We must choose to expectantly wait for God to work in our lives and trust that he is there even when it feels like nothing is happening.

True faith is not passive but active, and genuinely active faith requires focusing on the health of our entire being—spiritually and physically. As we discussed in Chapter Two, 1 Corinthians 3:16 reminds us that we are God's temples, and stress can tear down that temple from the inside out. By nurturing our faith and staying in tune with our bodies, we will be ready spiritually and physically to move with him when the time is right and according to his will. If any part of the temple is broken or not cared for, consequences will eventually appear.

Your Body Can Talk

Turning our problems over to God and trusting he loves us, remembers us, sees our issues, and desires to intervene in our lives in his perfect timing are pivotal in our quest to find less stress and more peace. But, in the meantime, we cannot afford to ignore physical warnings of destruction. Our bodies give us plenty of warning signs to let us know when our stress is pushing us into the danger zone, but all too often we turn a blind eye to what's really happening. Nobody knows your body as well as you do, so once you learn to identify your own signs of stress, they can serve as your personal emergency broadcast system.

Hypothetically, consider your body is an expensive, high-end car with a shiny exterior and all the finest bells and whistles. Since you have a lot invested in this car and want to keep it running properly, you know you have to keep a keen eye on the dashboard gauges, as they are your only way to know what's going on under the hood. Even when things look perfectly normal and flawless on the outside, there could be engine problems or other issues that you only learn about because of the lights and alarms the car provides to alert you that attention is needed.

Our body has gauges too, as well as alarms, although our alarms do not exhibit themselves with sounds or blinking lights. While we would never ignore an obvious problem with our vehicle that could possibly cause us to be stranded on the side of the road, we are quick to ignore alarms that our body is sending—writing them off as more of a nuisance than an actual problem demanding our attention. However, ignoring these issues can cause us to become stranded along the highway of life and to possibly face a major, costly repair job—or maybe even cost us our life. Yet if we are paying attention to what our bodies are telling us, we can quickly tend to a problem when it arises in the hopes of warding off future problems.

So what are the warning signs you should be looking for? How do you know if stress is taking a physical toll on you? How do you know if a health problem you've begun experiencing is related to stress or something else? Those warning signs vary from person to person. I have shared with you many of the symptoms that I experienced, but it certainly was not an all-inclusive list, because everyone's body reacts differently to stress. So let's talk about some of the most common symptoms.

Some symptoms of chronic stress issues could include things like changes in body functions; deterioration of your physical health; changes in moods, feelings, and emotions; crying at unusual times or over minor things; behavioral changes; increasing health issues; fatigue; inability to take deep breaths; irritability or increased anger;

changes in eating habits; inability to sleep soundly; increased use of drugs or alcohol; abuse of prescription drugs; withdrawal from friends or family members; an inability to concentrate; and feeling hopeless or helpless.

A few more bothersome problems include headaches, stomach problems, muscle tension, teeth grinding, changes in sex drive, dizziness, feeling nervous or anxious all the time, severing relationships, and having a lack of energy.[9]

Unfortunately, stress can and will affect every aspect of our lives, at times ushering in irreparable damage and consequences. For example, a family lawyer interviewed for an article on WebMD shared that although stress has always been a factor in marriages, sales of online self-help divorce agreements that teach people how to go about getting a divorce without hiring an expensive lawyer rose by 34 percent within a few months of the COVID-19 pandemic. In addition, over the course of a year, the family lawyers surveyed noted a 25 percent to 35 percent increase in divorce filings compared to the same time frame in 2019. Most of the divorce cases stemmed from stress-induced negative behaviors of married partners during the pandemic, such as the use of pornography, substance abuse, and infidelity.[10]

Parenting is hard enough, but add a pandemic; forced homeschooling; the inability to enjoy graduations, birthday parties, and sports events; social distancing; economic worries; and too much pressure to try to do it all, and it's a sure recipe for toxic stress—not only for the parents and their children, but on the parent–child relationship as well.

According to a 2020 report from Ann Arbor from the University of Michigan, parents reported high levels of psychological and physical punishment of children. Twenty percent reported having spanked or slapped children at least once over the past two weeks, and 11 percent had done so several times. Meanwhile, 41 percent of parents said they shouted, yelled, or screamed at children a few times or more in the past 2 weeks. Even if this out of the norm for most of the parents surveyed, their extenuating circumstances causing such inner turmoil and stress pushed them to the breaking point, and unfortunately, all too often, children take the brunt of our stress. Around 55 percent of parents who participated in this study said they were worried money would run out, and 50 percent were worried that they would not be able to afford their bills or support their families. Furthermore, 52 percent said financial stresses were interfering with their parenting, and 50 percent said social isolation was.[11]

If you're a parent, especially of young children, you know what it is to be stressed and you may even have some regrets of your own for how your stress provoked you to treat your children in ways that broke your heart afterward. It's okay, sweet friend—we've all been there. Apologize, hug your children, and forgive yourself, but let this be one of those warning signs that a problem is stirring and change is needed.

Workplace stress is another huge epidemic in our country, due to high job demands, deadlines, extended working hours, lack of control over career moves, workplace bullying, and even poor work environments. And within the past year, for those who didn't lose their employment due to pandemic-related business shutdowns and layoffs, workloads have increased, catapulting the stress levels of most individuals even higher. A recent article from the *Corporate Wellness Magazine* stated the effects of workplace stress can negatively impact an employee's performance but can also be detrimental to their physical and mental health. In response to workplace stressors, the body can experience elevated blood pressure and anxiety, all of which increase the chance of developing coronary heart disease, heart attacks, and strokes. The article also stated there was growing evidence that work-related stress increased the risk of developing diabetes, immune deficiency disorders, chronic back pain, other muscle and skeletal disorders, and gastrointestinal disorders such as irritable bowel syndrome. To make matters worse, aside from the physical consequences of stress breaking the body down, it can break us down mentally.[12]

Stress causes us to have more anxiety, burnout, and depression. It prompts us to abuse substances we've never turned to before, like drinking, drugs, overeating, or smoking, all because we are desperately searching for relief from our stress. All of this leads to higher health-care costs incurred by employees and employers alike.

Are you beginning to agree that stress is one of the worst epidemics to ever hit this country and the only life-threatening disease that is outright and purposely ignored? Isn't it amazing that an epidemic of these proportions is accepted as the norm and overlooked by everyone, including the people who are suffering the most? Isn't it even scarier that over the past couple of years, in the unprecedented times we've been living in, with all the added stressors in our lives due to the coronavirus, economic fallout, and political upheavals, people are still taking stress for granted, ignoring the warning signs, and failing to see the importance of regaining control over their lives and not intentionally pursuing the peace God so lovingly wants to provide? People from all over the world have taken precautions and gone to great lengths to protect ourselves from contracting a virus we can't control, yet we willingly choose to spend no effort or time to reduce our stress levels—which we *do* have control over—even though these stress levels could have the same fatal consequences as the global pandemic we're battling.

When we are operating in a constant high-stress mode, we may experience one bothersome symptom or an entire slew of them, but none of them should be ignored. I know myself well enough now to be able to recognize when stress is rearing its ugly head again, and I trust that soon you will also start listening to your body more closely and be on alert for your own warning signs before it's too late. If you don't want to do this for yourself, do it for those you love.

Fortunately, there is a vaccine for this disease of stress that can not only treat the majority of the symptoms but also potentially prevent them from occurring. It is a vaccine of hope found right smack in the middle of the words of Jesus Christ. When we inject these life-saving truths into our hearts, allowing them to course through our veins with healing strength, we will begin to see the life-changing power the Bible really holds.

Troubles and Treasures

Although my divorce from my husband was finalized several years ago, I vividly remember the painful memories of the earlier years of our marriage, which were often plagued with difficulties.

Despite the endless hours of prayer for my marriage, it felt as if my prayers were going nowhere. I was in a season of faith where I could relate to Hannah, wondering if God even remembered I was still down here on earth and if he cared about my pain at all. I had been praying for an improved marriage year after year, and for my husband to love me and for us to find happiness together, and I honestly was growing weary of the wait and tired of the battle.

One particular day, after another round of arguments due to a new and upsetting issue that had come to my attention due to some of my husband's choices and behaviors, I found myself in the deepest pit of despair I could remember ever being in at the time. I felt hurt and betrayed, and my trust was shaken; my mind and my heart raged with a flurry of anger and fears. No matter how hard I tried to talk about situations, all attempts would be met with the silent treatment, a smirk as if I were crazy, or an argument that would go sideways and somehow get twisted around to reverse blame and deny fault. Communication efforts had become more and more futile, resulting in not only more stress and frustration but deeper brokenheartedness and helplessness. I had no idea how to handle, much less fix, the issues that now threatened our relationship, and my stress and anxiety were through the roof, to the point of making me feel physically ill.

One rainy Sunday afternoon, shortly after this new and troubling issue had presented itself in our lives, I found myself feeling extremely sad, worried, discouraged, hopeless, and afraid. It seemed like all the problems in the world were crashing down upon me all at once. I felt a weight so heavy on my heart, as if I could barely stand. But, as a mother of three young children who were upstairs in their rooms within earshot of any conversation, I had no choice but to bury my emotions and keep up the all-too-familiar charade that *everything was fine.*

I knew that, for the sake of my family, it would be inappropriate to have a meltdown, wallow in a puddle of tears, yell, or bang my fists on the floor. Letting my emotions explode, even if they were warranted, would not only upset the children but would have resulted in a whole new set of issues and broken hearts to deal with. But burying our stress and emotions rather than dealing with them is like pouring lighter fuel on a pile of smoldering logs.

The gloomy, rainy day had trapped us all inside, and everyone was occupied with toys and television in their own little spaces in the house. So I wandered into the solace of my bedroom and quietly closed the door. The room was unusually dark for the time of day it was, so I clicked on the lamp beside my bed. As the warm glow bathed the room in soft light, my eyes landed upon the gift that a precious Christian friend had given me just a few weeks earlier.

It was a small crystal box engraved with delicate designs, including a little heart right on the top, still snuggled in the puffy, yellow chiffon bow that had been lovingly placed around it. Some people have called it a "treasure box," others a "blessings box," but no matter what you call it, it had become a heartfelt keepsake. Although it was a beautiful addition to my bedside table, it wasn't the physical beauty of the box that mattered at all but the beauty of the contents inside that I truly treasured.

This little glass box was filled with dozens of small, carefully folded slips of paper, and on each slip of paper was written an encouraging Bible verse. This would have been a wonderful gift in itself, but, to make it even more special, my friend had inserted my name into each of the verses so that when I read each verse, it was as if God were speaking directly to me. As if he were calling out to Tracie by name with his individual promises of hope, love, compassion, and peace.

Sitting quietly on my bed, away from the eyes of my husband and little ones, I allowed the tears that I had been holding in ever so tightly to escape. After the first tear fell, many followed suit. I sobbed for a few minutes into my pillow, feeling lost, hopeless, and incredibly alone. I pleaded for God to help me, to take away my pain, to tell me what to do, and to help me have peace—even when it seemed impossible. I didn't know how much more stress I could take.

I suddenly felt a nudge from the Holy Spirit to pick up the box. I wiped my eyes and placed it on the bed in front of me. I carefully untied the yellow bow, removed the fragile lid, and slowly began to unfold each little slip of paper—something I hadn't fully done since I'd received the gift. As I read each verse silently, I began asking God to hear my prayers, comfort me, take away my hurt, and show me the way. For the very first time, I completely surrendered my situation and my stress, asking for his peace to overwhelm my broken heart.

I again felt like Hannah. I thought about how her desperate plea to God was worded perfectly for my situation, especially as it is translated in *The Message* Bible: "Oh, GOD-of-the-Angel-Armies, If you'll take a good, hard look at my pain, If you'll quit neglecting me and go into action for me" (1 Sam. 1:11).

Hannah's words echoed the emotions that were bubbling in my heart like boiling water at peak temperature. I wanted God to see me sitting in my bedroom all alone with swollen red eyes and a broken heart. I wanted him to quit neglecting me and my pleas for a happy marriage and a faithful husband. I wanted him to take some action and do something, for goodness sake! I knew he had the power, so why had he not intervened? Why was he allowing this suffering to come upon us and plague us for years? Ashamedly, I began to doubt his ways, as my emotional exhaustion permeated my soul.

Since I was being honest with God, I felt this was the prime opportunity to remind him that, although I wasn't perfect by any means, I was trying to live a life that would glorify him. I did try to be a good Christian, a good wife, a good mother, and a good follower of his Word. I had followed his call to become a speaker and a writer. I had made sacrifices to carry out his will for my life. So why couldn't he just make this all better? In fact, why didn't he prevent this situation from happening altogether? Why would he allow me to come under this level of stress again?

And, friends, I'm just going to be honest with you. I was mad at God for not protecting me and for not keeping his hand on my marriage. I was frustrated with him for not answering my prayers and seemingly ignoring them altogether. If you have ever felt so frustrated with God's seeming lack of concern for your most heart-wrenching problems, I know you can relate.

As I continued to sit there on my crumpled covers, my deepest thoughts, hurts, anger, and fears shoved their way to the surface with torrential force, and I could no longer hold it all in. I fell over and buried my head in my pillow and let it all out, while beginning a time of intense prayer and focus. Just like Hannah, I had nothing left to give at this point. I could not fix our problems, and nothing I said or did mattered. I had no option left but to pray and seek God's presence with my whole heart. I was weak and I knew I needed his strength to go on.

Snuggled in God's Lap

After what seemed like an eternity in silent, fervent prayer, I knew I was no longer alone. I felt him move in my spirit, and his presence hovered around me. Spiritual chill bumps covered my body from head to toe. Although my eyes could not see him, my heart knew he was there. I could sense him wrapping his big, fatherly, comforting arms around me and pulling me into his presence. And you know what? I really needed a hug right then and there.

But he didn't stop there. He began whispering to my heart as I sat there in acute awareness of the presence of God. Then, suddenly, an idea popped into my mind that could have only come from God. I would have never thought of doing something quite this bizarre on my own accord.

God's quiet whisper said, *Tracie, lay the verses from the box all around you. Trust me.*

I pondered that thought for a moment, thinking it sounded a little fanatical and weird. I wondered what someone would think if they came into my bedroom and saw me swimming in my bed in a sea of little papers. I could envision the wide-eyed looks of my children if they were to pounce into my bedroom and interrupt this private moment, concluding that Mommy had finally gone off the deep end.

But in a split second, God recaptured my attention and I realized that, in that moment, nothing else mattered but him. My spirit quickened and my heart began to beat faster as I felt him nudging me to obey this simple request. So, instead of glancing at a couple of verses and then putting them back into the box, as I normally did, I proceeded to take them all out and spread them around me on the bed.

I laid most of the verses directly in front of me, so my eyes could wander over the words of comfort they held, allowing his precious peace to saturate my soul as I read each one over and over. I placed several verses to my right and several to my left. Then, hesitantly, and feeling a little silly, I turned around and laid a few of them behind me, propping them up on my soggy pillow that had been used as a tear catcher just a few moments earlier. I paused and looked at what I had done.

As I sat on my bed, fully surrounded on every side by holy Words and divine promises inscribed with my name, I heard these words wash through my spirit, *Sweet child, you are now sitting in my lap.*

I was sitting in God's lap? My heart skipped a beat. The thought of it nearly took my breath away. It was only then that I realized I *was* sitting in the comforting, safe lap of my Heavenly Father, who loved me enough to hold me. God *had* seen me in my bedroom and had reached down to hold me, his little girl.

What an indescribable privilege to know God had invited me to not only sit with him but to be nestled into his holy lap. To be tucked in the middle of his comforting words. To be in the presence of the most high and sovereign God. To be hugged by the One who gave me life. The One who remembered me. The One who loved me. The One who could comfort me. The One who had never neglected me but had simply waited patiently for me to acknowledge my need for him and invite him to take control of my circumstance.

I cannot explain the astonishing peace that came over me at that moment. It was a peace that flooded my heart as I felt the power of his written promises, specifically *for* Tracie and *to* Tracie, sprinkled all around me. The weight of the stress suffocating me before I walked into that bedroom seemed to be lifted.

My spirit leapt as I realized I was no longer merely surrounded by typed slips of paper; I was surrounded by countless reassurances that God had heard my prayers. He was not neglecting me, nor had he forgotten me. In fact, he was sitting on the bed with me, holding my heart and catching every tear, just as we are told he does in Psalm 56:8: "You keep track of all my sorrows. You have collected all my tears in your bottle. You have recorded each one in your book."

God embraced this opportunity, when the wounds of my heart were bleeding profusely, to gently and lovingly remind me that he loved me enough to show himself in a way that I could feel and understand. He loved me enough to bring me peace. All I had to do was say those two little words that he loved to hear, *"Yes, Lord,"* and accept the gift he was offering.

After that life-changing encounter with God, I knew I had to let go of the steering wheel of my marriage and allow God to take over. I put my full trust in him. I agreed to wait, no matter how long it took, to see how he would work.

The tears began to flow again. But this time, they were tears of relief and gratitude and joy . . . but most of all, peace. I had entered into a holy place when I walked into the confines of my bedroom, and I walked out a new person. I vowed to trust God's ways, even if I did not understand them or like them. I had to be willing to wait for God's best even though the waiting period would be difficult.

The difference between this waiting period and the wait I had already been enduring was I was no longer *hoping* that he would see me, *wishing* that he would work, or *wondering* if he would care. Instead, I *knew* he heard my prayers, he saw me, and he loved me.

My marriage circumstances did not change that day, and although my husband and I remained married for several years after my encounter with God, eventually the ongoing patterns of behavior and infidelity caused irreparable damage, to the point where reconciliation was not possible. But even in the midst of the devastation of separation and divorce, and living in the wake of the destruction of the end of my twenty-five-year marriage, God never failed to fill me with peace upon every ask.

God always has a plan and a purpose. We can trust him to carry us through any situation and give us the peace we need to persevere, hang onto hope, and embrace and enjoy the life we are living—even if it's not the life we once imagined.

As you can imagine, my divorce journey was laced with great stress. I regressed back to a state of damaging my physical health due to the level of sadness, anger, fear, and anxiety that plagued my every waking moment. My mental health was unwell, and I took up some bad habits as coping mechanisms. But once again, I was aware of what my body was telling me, because God had been teaching me how to manage my stress for many, many years, and this opportunity called me to apply what I had learned. The day came when I was tired of being sick and tired, unhealthy and miserable. I decided to regain control of my life and my stress. And despite your situation right now, you can do the same exact thing—if only you choose to do so and care enough about yourself, your life, and your loved ones to finally make it a priority.

Our Flawless Role Model

Everyone experiences stress, even Jesus did. However, when we look at the abundant life he led as he walked on earth as a man, we see Jesus was never in a hurry. He was never worried about his reputation or the gossip or slander people were saying behind his back. I cannot recall any situations in the Bible where Jesus seemed frazzled or disheveled, running around frantically, trying to get everything done on his daily to-do lists, yelling at people out of impatience, or losing his temper when he felt overburdened in some way. And when he did have to deal with people in conflict situations, he handled them with love, gentleness, self-control, and patience. Even in his anger, he did not sin. First Peter 2:21–24 offers a glimpse of how Jesus handled himself in a time of excessive stress:

> For God called you to do good, even if it means suffering, just as Christ suffered for you. He is your example, and you must follow in his steps. He never sinned, nor ever deceived anyone. He did not retaliate when he was insulted, nor threaten revenge when he suffered. He left his case in the hands of God, who always judges fairly. He personally carried our sins in his body on the cross

so that we can be dead to sin and live for what is right.
By his wounds you are healed.

Jesus suffered at the hands of others, yet he did not sin. He suffered without being filled with thoughts of revenge and retaliation. He suffered without pointing fingers. He even prayed for his enemies, including those who were mercilessly persecuting him. He suffered without questioning the reason why he had to suffer.

Despite his pain, Jesus knew if something was happening, it was the will of his Father. So, even at his lowest point, he willingly took on the punishment of the world with gentleness and grace.

Hebrews 2:18 tells us that because he physically experienced what we go through on this earth, he is able to come to our rescue when we are feeling like we can't take anymore: "Since he himself has gone through suffering and testing, he is able to help us when we are being tested." The New International Version Bible translates it this way: "Because he himself suffered when he was tempted, he is able to help others who are being tempted." No one is immune to the temptation of worry and stress—they are a fact of life and a test of our faith. Although Jesus would prefer we trust him fully in all things, he understands our weaknesses and is available to help us persevere.

In my case, however, I seem to handle suffering a little less gracefully than Jesus. There are countless days when I find myself frazzled, disheveled, and worried. Unfortunately, on these days when I am most stressed and distressed, those adjectives describing Jesus's behavior are not words that would typically describe me. My normal way of handling stressful circumstances would not be characterized by love, calmness, self-control, or patience. Even after many years of praying to God for a sweet and gentle spirit, stress can still bring out the worst in me!

Clearly, we will never be able to handle stress with holiness as well as Jesus did, because well, he's Jesus. We will never be immune to the temptations of reacting to stress in negative ways, but we can rest in knowing Jesus understands our shortcomings. Lamentations 3:23 reassures us his mercies are renewed every morning. He knows we can never be just like him, but he encourages each of us to give it our best shot by following his lead, depending on his peace to reside in our hearts so when stressful situations hit—and they always will—we will be ready.

No matter how long we have been a believer, if our hearts are not in the right place with God, peace will always seem just out of reach. We can believe every word in the Bible is flawless and be at church every time the doors open, yet still not allow his Word to shape our lives or impact our thoughts and behaviors (or our stress levels), keeping us from basking in his peace on a daily basis.

I once heard a story about an elderly lady in my home church who had served in our congregation for dozens of years. One Sunday, in the midst of a powerful sermon, God broke through her mask and penetrated her heart for the very first time. She realized she had never really accepted Jesus as her personal Savior but had only been going through the motions of being a "good Christian." She was physically engaged but spiritually disconnected from the Jesus she was worshipping. How sad it is that she spent most of her life not enjoying the peace that surpasses all understanding. A true relationship with Christ is what we all need to manifest the patient and peaceful character traits of God within us when we are faced with major stressors.

Once we are fully connected with Jesus, we will begin craving an insatiable daily portion of him to nourish our souls and fill our spirits with the peace we are starving for.

Craving a Daily Portion

If the phrase "you are what you eat" were literally true, my son would have turned into a bowl of chocolate ice cream when he was little. Before he was even old enough to say "ice cream," he loved it—but only chocolate.

Once when little Michael was four years old, he pleaded in his sweet little-boy voice for some chocolate ice cream. "Pleeeaaassseeeee, Mommy," he said with blue eyes bulging and bottom lip poked out for sympathy's sake. I could never say no to such an adorable face (and he was fully aware of my weakness), so I agreed and pulled the gallon of ice cream out of the freezer. I pried open the lid and realized it was nearly empty, so rather than exhaust my arm muscles trying to scoop and scoop and scoop to get that little bit of hard ice cream out, I told Michael to just get a spoon and eat it straight out of the gallon. I created a monster that day.

Once he discovered eating out of the gallon meant his portion would not be limited to the few scoops I put into a bowl, life changed as he knew it. Never again did he ask for ice cream without taking a shot at proposing he eat out of the gallon.

In the same way, we should never want our portion of God to be limited. If we are spiritually connected to God, we will have a hunger for him that can never be satisfied—always harboring a longing for more of his Word and a desire for unlimited portions. Psalm 73:26 says, "My flesh and my heart may fail, but God is the strength of my heart and my portion forever" (NIV).

This verse refers to "portion" to describe how although we will fail, God is enough to make up for our human-ness. God offers us the exact portion of him that we need to get through life—if we are hungry enough to ask for it and seek it out. What a blessing it is to know we can "eat out of the gallon" of God's Word (with the advantage of not having to worry about calories).

We all need a portion of his peace every day, and it can be ours if we stay plugged into the One who is dishing it out.

ᘎ Reflection Questions

1. What childhood memories come to mind that bring back feelings of peace and joy? How can you tap into those feelings of positive times to help you cope during difficult times?

What memories come to mind that conjure up feelings of stress or anxiety? If there are stressful memories that are possibly keeping you from embracing peace and joy in Christ, take a moment to talk them over with God. Ask him to help you forget the past and focus on all the good things he has for your future. Write out a heartfelt prayer asking for his clarity in understanding why you are allowing these issues to be a part of your life and to help you let the past be the past—forgiven and forgotten.

2. How are you like Hannah in the Bible? In what ways can her trust and devotion to God be motivation for you to reach out to God with your most difficult problems or deepest unmet desires?

3. Circle any of the physical problems below that you have experienced lately.

Fatigue	Headache	Upset stomach
Muscle tension	Teeth grinding	Change in sex drive
Dizziness	Irritability	Anger
Nervousness	Lack of energy	Quick to cry
Change in appetite	Unexplained health issues	

Consider if any of the problems you circled could possibly be stress related. What changes can you implement in your life today to reduce your stress for the sake of improving your health?

Consider writing your suggested areas of change on a note card and hang it on your mirror, refrigerator, or anywhere you will take notice of it each day to remind you of your commitment to yourself and your health.

4. Have you been feeling like God is absent lately? Are you just going through the motions, instead of really worshipping him? Is it possible that you have been disconnected or unplugged from God? What can you do to plug into God?

5. Write a brief prayer below about an issue you have been asking for God's help on for a long time but God has yet to answer. Then write a promise to God that you will trust him and his timing.

Prayer:

Commitment Promise:

6. Do you believe that your life would improve if you developed an insatiable craving for a portion of God's Word every day? What are three steps you can take toward this goal? How do you think meeting these goals will impact your faith level and your relationship with Christ?

7. How do you normally handle stressful situations? Is it possible that your reactions to stress could be causing additional problems in your relationships and life in general? Write down three improvements you would like to make with regards to how you react to stressful situations.

Stress-Busting Scriptures

God's whole nature is living in Christ in human form.
Because you belong to Christ, you have everything you need.
He is the ruler over every power and authority.

Colossians 2:9–10 NIrV

We are God's creation. He created us to belong to Christ Jesus.
Now we can do good works.
Long ago God prepared these works for us to do.

Ephesians 2:10 NIrV

Hatred stirs up quarrels, but love makes up for all offenses.

Proverbs 10:12

The LORD replied, "My Presence will go with you,
and I will give you rest."

Exodus 33:14 NIV

Trust in the LORD and do good. Then you will live safely in the land
and prosper. Take delight in the LORD, and he will give you your
heart's desires. Commit everything you do to the LORD.
Trust him, and he will help you.

Psalm 37:3–5

Bonus:
✍ Quiet Time Activity

Could you use some snuggle time in God's lap? Would you like to spend some time sitting in the middle of God's Word? Below is a list of Bible verses that were included in my blessings box from my friend LeAnn, which blessed me with the opportunity to sit in God's lap.

In order to make your own blessings box, type each Bible verse into a document, and insert your name into each one. You may also want to include any verses that are special to your heart as well, and consider creating a paraphrased version in which you can insert your name in a personal way. Then print out the verses and individually cut them apart. You can put the verses in a dainty bowl, a beautiful glass box, or a paper cup—what's important is that you have them available.

Find a quiet place to spend some time with God, and strategically place the verses all around you. You could retreat to your bedroom as I did or any place that provides privacy and solace. Invite God into your heart and into your life, opening the door for him to make his presence known to you. Focus on talking with him in prayer as if he were sitting right in front of you, while remembering that as soon as you invite him in, he will be there with you.

(Your name here), I carry your burdens every day. Psalm 68:19

You can know and depend on the love that I have for you, (_____). 1 John 4:16

You can trust in my faithfulness, (_____), because my Word is true. Psalm 33:4

If you enter in my rest, (_____), you will find rest from all your striving. Hebrews 4:9–10

My Spirit will help you in your weakness, (_____). Romans 8:26

You can rest in my love, (_____), for I have power to save you. Zephaniah 3:17

I will meet your every need, (_____), through my eternal riches in Jesus Christ. Philippians 4:19

I will be the voice behind you, (_____), guiding you in the way you should go. Isaiah 30:21

(_____), I will give you power to know the vastness of my immeasurable love. Ephesians 3:17–19

Trust in me with all your heart, (_____), and I will guide you. Proverbs 3:5–6

Come close to me, (_____), and I will come close to you. James 4:8

I prepared a kingdom inheritance for you, (_____), when I created the world. Matthew 25:34

I am with you, (_____), and I will help you because I am your God. Isaiah 41:10

My promise of life is for you and for your family, (_____). Acts 2:39

Reach out and you will touch me, for I am not far from you, (_____). Acts 17:27

Commit all that you do to me, (_____), and your plans will be successful. Proverbs 16:3

You can trust in me, (_____), for I am your strength and your song. Isaiah 12:2

I will never abandon you, (_____). Hebrews 13:5

If you wait for me, (_____), I will work on your behalf.
Isaiah 64:4

An eternal crown awaits you at the finish line, (_____).
1 Corinthians 9:24–25

I am near to you whenever you cry out, (_____).
Deuteronomy 4:7

I will keep watch over you and guard you forever, (_____).
Psalm 12:7

My love will never fail you, (_____). 1 Corinthians 13:8

Call on me, (_____), when you are in trouble and I will rescue
you. Psalm 91:15

There is no place you can go to escape my presence, (_____).
Psalm 13:7–10

When problems arise, (_____), call to me and I will answer you.
Psalm 86:7

The good things I have planned for you, (_____), are too many
to count. Psalm 40:5

For you, (_____), are honored in my eyes. I, your God, am
your strength. Isaiah 49:5

I will protect and carry you, (_____), all the days of your life.
Isaiah 46:4

Though the mountains vanish, my unending love will never leave
you, (_____). Isaiah 54:10

Ask me for wisdom, (_____), and I will generously give it to you.
James 1:5

(_____), I have a special plan and purpose for your life. Seek
hope in me. Jeremiah 29:11

CHAPTER SIX

Overcoming Your Giants

Our problems and stressors can sometimes seem so much bigger than we can handle, especially when we are not only facing one giant problem but many. You may be facing a major giant right now—being in a personal relationship that has suffered many blows, a struggling marriage, a spouse addicted to pornography, a friend or family member held hostage by substance abuse or maybe even your own addiction, an inability to find employment despite searching for months, home foreclosure, difficult bosses, loss of loved ones, harassing credit and collection phone calls, tragic accidents, chronic or terminal illness, family problems, or sexual or physical abuse. There are lots of giants in our lives, especially with the added stressor of living in the thick of a global pandemic, which seems like an invisible giant wreaking havoc on our lives, filling us with fear, and rendering us helpless to control it.

While I was walking through all the twists and turns of my divorce journey, battling my giant, I leaned on God like never before. Each breath seemed like an impossible task. Depression set in and was taking its toll. My bank account was depleted, and I still had three children to take care of. Loneliness filled my soul. An ache for what could have been lingered daily. The future seemed like the scariest thing to think about, and hopelessness had become my most constant companion. But over the course of several years, I watched God intervene in situations that had no other explanation but his divine work in my life. When I received unexpected financial support out of the blue in a myriad of ways at exactly the time I needed it; when I found healing and hope, even in the midst of devastation; when I was supported and encouraged by the people he had been placing in my life for years for such a time as this—my faith soared. I've never seen God at work so clearly as when my stress level pushed me to the point of desperation for his peace that surpassed understanding.

Even today as I write this, I continue to fight exhausting, seemingly hopeless legal battles for issues that I was not involved with but am suffering the consequences of, due to being married to the man responsible. It isn't fair that I need to fight these legal battles, and practically every month, another hurdle pops up that I need to try to figure out how to climb over, Yet, despite a sense of hopelessness always threatening my peace, giant problems which seem impossible to battle, I still notice I can fight that temptation of letting stress rob my peace by capturing my negative thoughts and redirecting them to something more positive. I have learned that I can still maintain a peace within myself that can only be explained by the presence of the Holy Spirit in my heart, regardless of what is happening around me.

This is not to say I don't have my meltdown moments and occasional anxiety attacks—I am only human, and there is a limit to how much one person can take without snapping and losing it. And that's okay. But, in general, God's peace has carried me through situations I otherwise would have never made it through sanely. And that peace, my friend, can be yours too. Can you even imagine how wonderful it would feel to face tomorrow feeling free from the chokehold of stress and totally equipped to handle whatever the day throws at you?

As we become more mature in faith, learning to trust God is capable of all things, including winning the battle against the giants in our lives, we are able to keep even our biggest stressors from sending us into a tailspin because we know he is capable of handling them. Then each time he intervenes in our lives, witnessing his power and the reality of his actual presence, our love and trust for him grow and we begin to realize he really is true to his Word—that peace is not just a fantasy emotion that only happens to lucky people who don't have any real problems in their lives. Once we allow ourselves to grasp how capable God really is of handling all our problems, we can learn to put aside worry and rest in knowing that he knows what to do and his plans are good—leaving no need for us to destroy ourselves by stressing over them.

By the grace of God alone, I feel so blessed to have discovered years ago that regardless of my circumstances, I do not have to let stress run my life. God never intended for us to lead lives buried in despair, anxiety, and dread. He never meant for us to be so bogged down with worry and stress we would dread getting up in the morning; although, this type of living became a reality when sin came into his perfect world. But God is still God. We cannot escape our lives, but he is our escape from stress.

Out of curiosity, I polled a few of my Facebook friends to ask what giants they were facing right now, causing them the most stress and anxiety, and their answers varied. Here are just a few:

- Isolation due to COVID restrictions. As a widow, I thrive on human contact.
- I'm afraid of getting the virus.
- I wonder if freedom will ever be a part of our history again.
- My children losing the experience of actually being able to go to school.

- I have a brain tumor, but due to restrictions I can't see my family right now.
- I'm out of work and desperately need a job so I can get a place of my own.
- The newly elected president and worrying about what the future holds.
- I recently lost my husband, and now I have to move out of my home.
- My daughter just told me she is pregnant and in a toxic relationship.
- I was just diagnosed with Parkinson's.
- Being at home all day with my children—caring for their needs, homeschooling, working freelance. I never get a break, and there is no "me time."
- News and social media cause me so much anxiety that I have trouble sleeping.
- Going through a nasty divorce and enduring the hateful things my husband is doing to me and my children.

I imagine you could add a few of your own bullet points here. We all could. Those who were courageous enough to share their experiences with us certainly have giants looming large in their lives. Giant problems. Giant fears. Giant anxiety provokers. Giant joy stealers. But then I followed up on my original post and asked my friends what they were doing to try to keep their stress at bay. Their answers included the following:

- Walking around a lake in our town while praying and reflecting.
- Intentionally trying to focus on who God is, what he can do, and his promises.
- Spending hours in the Word, leading virtual Bible groups, running three times a week.

- Writing devotionals and spending time in Bible study, prayer, and praise. Also, talking to my mom, who is a strong believer. Asking others to pray for me and my children.
- Having conversations with God, along with intentional prayer and fasting.
- Listening to Christian music all day.
- Putting more focus on what I eat, getting out of the house to go for walks, and always spending time with God's Word.

I found it so interesting the majority of responses were faith based. I think today's unprecedented times have pushed people to the point of needing God's peace more than ever before. So many have realized that while there is so much in life that is out of *our* hands, all of life is in *God's* hands. It's almost as if a paradigm shift of thinking has taken place in the silent majority of the population, and people are realizing God is the only solution to the stress caused by the giants in our lives.

Overcoming your stress begins with recognizing the fact that no matter what problems are causing you stress and anxiety, it is possible to have peace if you change your pattern of thinking and believe that no matter what, God has things under control. I know it's not easy, because our patterns of thinking have developed over a lifetime and likely been shaped by our experiences, but it is possible if living the stress-less life is something you are willing to work for.

Romans 12:2 says: "Do not conform any longer to the pattern of this world, but be transformed by the renewing of your mind. Then you will be able to test and approve what God's will is—his good, pleasing and perfect will" (NIV). You see, changing your life begins in your mind. When you change the way you look at things, the things you look at will change. It's all about perspective. Perspective can open the door for peace to enter, or it can open the door for peace to escape.

Retraining your mind to change the way you think about your circumstances is a game changer and is the first step to opening our hearts to receive God's peace, which is his will for us, even in the midst of the less-than-peaceful circumstances of life.

The Power of Optimism

In my book *Unsinkable Faith: God-Filled Strategies for Transforming the Way You Think, Feel, and Live*, I shared three simple steps to forming a practice of renewing your mind, which also means changing your way of thinking. If put into practice every time you start thinking fretful, worrisome, or negative thoughts about whatever big or small giant you're facing, you can prevent stress from taking over.

There's a simple process you can remember called "The Three Rs": recognize, reject, and replace. The first step is to ask God to help you be aware of when your negative or worrisome thoughts are ramping up, so you can intentionally stop them in their tracks. Once you form a habit of recognizing when you're becoming consumed with negative, stress-inducing thoughts, only then can you take authority over them and make the intentional decision to think differently.

For example, during the first year of my separation from my husband, when all financial support abruptly ceased, finances became my biggest source of stress. Fear was as ever present as my heartbeat, and each passing day only made it worse. When a bill I wasn't expecting would arrive in the mail, when the mortgage payments got further and further behind, when the amount of bills to be paid far exceeded the amount of money in the bank account, worry and fear would keep me up for nights on end. I wasted countless days, weeks, and months crying, worrying, and stressing myself out to the point of weight loss and feeling physically ill. But it never failed—and I mean *never*. God always provided for my needs in miraculous ways I can't even begin to take the time to explain. I gradually learned that all the stressing in the world wasn't going to solve my problems or kill my giants, and I could live in peace despite those issues if I put my trust in God and believed he would be faithful to fight the battle for me. We can trust him with all our battles, no matter what they are, but that alone is a perspective shift we have to intentionally strive for. Forming a habit of recognizing when our thoughts are luring us into stress sets us up to begin making that shift.

The second step after you recognize a negative or stress-inducing thought is to reject it! We can't control what's happening around us or all of our circumstances, but we have complete control and authority over our own thoughts. No one can force us to think one way or another, so we have the power to choose to reject a negative or stress-inducing thought and choose to not let it affect our attitudes. If you recognize yourself thinking about something that makes you feel hopeless, worried, stressed, or afraid, say out loud to yourself, "Stop!" You could go as far as to say, "I rebuke you, negative thoughts! You will not get the better of me!" I know that sounds a little drastic. Or maybe even a little crazy. But you get the point. Don't let your thoughts run your life. When you reject negative, stressful thoughts, they lose their power over you.

And third, once you recognize the thoughts that are causing you stress and decide to reject them, try to replace them with something more positive. Give that thought a more positive twist, even if it seems impossible to think of something positive about a difficult situation or problem. For example, during my financial crisis, I often found myself thinking thoughts like *I'll never be able to survive on my own* and *I'll never find a job that will sufficiently support me and my children.* Those thoughts only served to send me deeper into depression and hopelessness. Once I made a habit of recognizing, rejecting, and replacing my negative patterns of thinking, my entire attitude and life changed.

I decided that every time those hopeless thoughts crept up again, I would take a deep breath and give myself a pep talk. *Tracie, don't say those negative things. Trust in your God. You will survive. You will find a good job. God is faithful.* If I woke up in the morning and the first thought that crossed my mind was *I don't think I can endure another day of loneliness and pain*, I would immediately shake it off and replace those thoughts with *I am so grateful to have been given another day to live, and I am going to trust God and seek his peace, no matter what this day holds.*

At first, trying to change your habitual way of thinking and retrain your brain to stop letting stressful, negative thoughts rule your life may feel awkward, forced, or even artificial. But as you continue to put these three Rs into practice, God's renewal and transformation of your mind will truly begin, you will experience a shift in perspective, and an attitude adjustment will be the best gift you've ever given yourself.

Maintaining a Christlike Attitude

A Christlike attitude—one that stays joyous and positive even in the midst of stressful circumstances and trusts that God is working even when it seems he is absent—is gradually built over a lifetime of submitting to God's desires over our own. Most people have at least one problem or worry that seems bigger than life. This problem may feel like a giant so large that you feel powerless to stand up and face it. If you feel like there is nothing you can do about the giants in your life, I want you to take a closer look at what those giants really are. I listed a few of the most common giants at the beginning of this chapter, all of which take an enormous toll on our hearts and drain our spirits. Maybe those are some of the giants you are facing today, and you may have some others to toss in the mix. But is the identifying label for the surface problem the actual problem?

Or does the problem lie in the underlying perceptions about those problems, instead?

Could it be that fear, doubt, insecurity, and not believing that God really sees you are adding to how big the problem seems? Could it be that the way you perceive the problem, deal with the problem, and live with the problem are actually part of the problem? Could it be that your attitude is one of the biggest giants you face, more so than the situation you are facing?

Our attitude is a major contributing factor to how we handle our problems and how we manage our stress. I know your problems are real. The circumstances may be scary and filling your heart with worry, and the outcome of the unknown may leave reason to be fearful. I am not downplaying the fact that true and overwhelming circumstances occur every day in our lives and that you may be hurting right now. I am simply suggesting we take a closer look at the real root of the stress and see if we can work through it so that you can become an overcomer.

Facing Your Giants

The first step to overcoming any giant is changing your thought patterns and perspectives, remembering that God is always in control, and then being willing to confront your giant face-to-face. The giant, whatever it is, is the only thing standing between you and victory. Victory in this case is defined by defeating stress.

In 1 Samuel 17, we learn about David and Goliath—a well-known story, with a well-known ending. But let's take a moment to dig a little deeper into what the real giant was for the army that stood helpless against the Philistines.

> The Philistines and Israelites faced each other on oppo-
> site hills, with the valley between them. Then Goliath,
> a Philistine champion from Gath, came out of the
> Philistine ranks to face the forces of Israel. He was

over nine feet tall! He wore a bronze helmet, and his bronze coat of mail weighed 125 pounds. He also wore bronze leg armor, and he carried a bronze javelin on his shoulder. The shaft of his spear was as heavy and thick as a weaver's beam, tipped with an iron spearhead that weighed 15 pounds. His armor bearer walked ahead of him carrying a shield. (vv. 3–7)

It was not necessarily this giant Philistine that made the Israelites feel hopeless about their victory. Instead, it was their attitude toward him. To the Israelites, it looked like there was no way to beat a creature of his stature and strength. Not only did they have this huge valley between themselves and the enemy but the enemy was also absolutely enormous. Can you imagine what he must have looked like based on the description we are given in the Bible?

If I had seen Goliath off in the distance, I probably would have reacted just like all the Israelites who stayed safely in their tents on their side of the valley, cowering in fear at the sight of this monstrosity of a person.

Yet, even though Goliath was huge and threatening, the Israelites still longed for victory. Even though they thought victory was impossible, they still dreamed about it. There are issues in my life that seem as if they will never end, but I still want them to. The problem for the Israelites was they couldn't envision victory because their eyes were focused on the problem—Goliath.

The fear that Goliath created in them caused them to adopt an attitude of defeat. They were defeated long before the battle actually took place. The real giant they needed to overcome was not the physical presence of Goliath, but the mental presence of stress, worry, and fear in their hearts.

Goliath stood and shouted a taunt across to the Israelites. "Why are you all coming out to fight?" he called. "I am the Philistine champion, but you are only the servants

of Saul. Choose one man to come down here and fight
me! If he kills me, then we will be your slaves. But if
I kill him, you will be our slaves! I defy the armies of
Israel today! Send me a man who will fight me!" When
Saul and the Israelites heard this, they were terrified and
deeply shaken. (1 Sam. 17:8–11)

There was no joy in the hearts of the Israelites after hearing what
Goliath had to say. They did not find his invitation amusing or inviting but so terrifying that it completely shook them up. Their defeat
not only seemed imminent but they knew that someone would have
to die and then they would all become slaves. Their fear not only
stemmed from the potential threat of immediate death, for which
no one wanted to volunteer, but also from imagining how horrible and tortuous daily life would be as servants of the Philistines.
Their fears were paralyzing; their situation seemed hopeless. And,
instead of calling out to God, even as their last resort, they hovered
helplessly in the shadows of their fear.

Their attitude was not focused on God. They didn't think to
call out to him for help. They didn't consider asking for a miracle,
much less expect one. Instead, their eyes were focused on the giant,
not on the God that had always been there for them. Just as we
often forget, it never even crossed their minds to ask God for help
in confronting their problem.

How often do you think we fall into that line of thinking? We
find ourselves in a difficult position, faced with hardships, challenges, and hopelessness, but instead of looking to the One that
could make a difference, we look at how big the problem is and
immediately begin spouting all the reasons why we cannot fight
that battle.

We search within our own knowledge base for answers. We
think we can do it by ourselves. We look to friends for advice. We
seek out family members for support. We turn to coworkers for

sympathy. We look to lawyers for justice. We look to counselors for therapy. We look to pastors for intercessory prayer. But we don't call out to God ourselves until we have exhausted every other possible avenue.

Victory does not merely come when the enemy is defeated but when we trust that God will have victory, no matter what our gut feelings are telling us. Real victory is when we learn to live with more joy and less stress, even when we can still see the giants looming off in the distance.

Goliath pranced in front of the Israelite army every morning and evening for forty days. It must have seemed to them that this problem would go on forever. But they were unaware that they would soon witness a miracle. David's father Jesse had eight sons, three of which were in Saul's army. After a while, Jesse sent David to go and check on his brothers, take them some grain and bread, and report back to him about how they were getting along.

First Samuel 17:20–23 says:

> So David left the sheep with another shepherd and set
> out early the next morning with the gifts, as Jesse had
> directed him. He arrived at the camp just as the Israelite
> army was leaving for the battlefield with shouts and
> battle cries. Soon the Israelite and Philistine forces stood
> facing each other, army against army. David left his
> things with the keeper of supplies and hurried out to the
> ranks to greet his brothers. As he was talking with them,
> Goliath, the Philistine champion from Gath, came out
> from the Philistine ranks. Then David heard him shout
> his usual taunt to the army of Israel.

One point that stands out to me about this passage is that as soon as David heard what was happening, he "hurried out" to the battlefield to meet his brothers. The NIV translation says he "ran to the battle lines." David did not look at the battle line from afar, measure the distance that he would have to run versus his own quickness and agility, contemplate specific rock-throwing moves, consider where he might be able to hide if things didn't work out, weigh all the positives against the negatives, or try to determine all the what-if scenarios so that he could be proactive and come up with solutions ahead of time. David just ran.

David did not hesitate in trusting God was bigger than the giant, and as a result, he stepped forward to confront Goliath with full confidence in God, not himself. We see him do this again after convincing his brothers that he was capable to fight the giant: "As Goliath moved closer to attack, David quickly ran out to meet him" (1 Sam. 17:48). Apparently, a lack of confidence was not something David struggled with, even though he was the baby in the family. But his confidence came from God—he knew that was all he needed to be strong.

So often our giants seem huge, especially when it comes to serious matters of life like finances, marriage, parenting, and health. The fear of these giants causes us to cower in the shadows, just like all those Israelites who saw their giant as a problem that could never be defeated. I have also found in my own experience that the longer I wait to confront a problem, the bigger that problem seems to get. But in any case, God is still bigger. Are you facing a giant today? Is this giant causing you stress? Does it appear to be growing larger the longer you ignore it? Do you desire to be an overcomer of this particular giant and your stress? Do you want to break free from negative thinking that steals your joy on a daily basis? Do you hunger for victory over stress?

What is really stopping you from running to the battle line? The giant problem itself, or a giant lack of faith? Is your *perspective* of the giant making you so stressed—more so than the problem itself? Is your attitude blocking your view of God and keeping peace too far away to grasp? These are hard questions to ask ourselves, but uncovering the root of the problem is like putting a stone in our slingshot and knowing God will use it in powerful ways to bring us the victory we so desire.

We usually want to see God at work before we will run to the battle line. We want the reward before we put up the sacrifice. But God wants us to make strides toward victory before he can do his best work—and victory begins when we are willing to run by faith, trusting he will lead the way.

When we change the way we think, we can change the way we feel and live, even if our circumstances remain the same, because a positive mind will always lead to a more positive, less stressed, and joy-filled life.

Learn to Run by Faith

The much-anticipated days of summer were finally here, and I was at my favorite place in the world—the beach. I hopped out of bed with an unusually eager attitude to do my morning exercise. As I stepped out of the door into the warm morning, seeing the sun rising in the sky and inhaling a deep breath of salty beach air, I immediately felt motivated to start my day. I headed for the soft sand. The subtle pounding of the waves hitting the shore sounded like music to my ears. I neared the edge of the surf and began jogging at a brisk pace.

After a short while, the morning sun became so exceptionally bright that it was hard to keep my eyes open at all. I reached for my sunglasses, which I thought were perched on my head, only to realize that in my haste to experience the beautiful Carolina surf I had left them behind.

Despite efforts to keep my eyes open, the brilliant sunshine straight in front of me across the vastness of the water was just too magnificent. I looked at the open area around me and decided it would be safe to go a short distance with my eyes closed completely. Knowing that miles of empty beach lay ahead of me and considering the fact that there were very few people at the beach this early in the morning, I closed my eyes tight and confidently ran forward. It was a strange feeling, one of vulnerability and slight concern, but, most importantly, one of trust. I had to trust that if I was going to run into anything or anyone, that someone would find it in their heart to warn me. Or at a minimum, not laugh when I plummeted face first into the sand.

But as I ran with my eyes closed, my heart opened wide and I began to pray. While talking with God, 2 Corinthians 5:7 came to mind: "We live by faith, not by sight" (NIV). Then a startling thought leapt into my mind: *I wonder if this is what God means when he tells us to walk by faith and not by sight?*

I allowed my mind to drift away from my surroundings and focus on this concept. In the case of my morning run, I already knew that there was nothing in my path to bump into. There were no people, dogs, umbrellas, or flying Frisbees out on the beach this early in the morning (especially since it was the middle of summer when most sane people were enjoying some extra sleep instead of sweating and panting on the sand at daybreak). So I felt completely confident running with my eyes closed.

However, life does not always have a clutter-free pathway for us to run on but is rather packed full of obstacles (a.k.a. giants). During my prayer time on this beautiful morning, I felt God nudging me to consider whether or not I would be willing to run with my eyes closed through the bumpy patches of life and solely rely on him, even when I did not know what lay in front of me. Would I be willing to trust God's guidance, even when my own eyes could plainly see the obstacles or giants in my way? Could I truly surrender my problems to him and let them go, and stop allowing worry to keep me up at night? Was I capable of trusting God with my life, circumstances, fears, and problems so much so that I literally wouldn't stress over them anymore? Oh glory day if that could actually happen.

I found myself asking God, *"Lord, please show me in which areas of my life I need to walk, and maybe run, by faith and not by sight. Where in my life do I not fully trust you?"*

For the next fifteen minutes, with each exhale of breath, God brought something or someone to mind that I needed to entrust to him—situations I had been stressing over and people I had been worried about. A family member's terminal illness. My sister's debilitating battle with multiple sclerosis and my broken heart over what the disease was doing to her body and her spirit. The impending death of my father due to cancer. A friend's slow-moving job search. A damaged relationship. A crumbling marriage due to infidelity and betrayal. That person I needed to forgive for hurting my feelings. Parenting concerns. Politics I didn't agree with. The future of our country. My own unknown future. My children's future. So many things that I spent so much energy and time worrying about, yet all things I had no power to fix or change, which only added more anxiety to my already burdened heart.

It became crystal clear to me in that moment that I was rarely walking by faith regarding issues of great concern in my life. I recognized that even those times when I may think I am walking hand in hand with God, I may still find myself hiding behind a tree, deathly afraid of the giants that lie ahead in the valley, and assuming that victory can never be mine.

I sometimes feel more like the Israelites did when facing Goliath than I would like to admit. I, too, am guilty of trying to figure out my own problems and carry my own burdens. I fret and worry. I imagine the worst-case scenario. I spend so much time thinking about troubling issues or circumstances, letting my thoughts run rampant toward all the terrible "what if" scenarios, that I end up with stomach pains and headaches. My personality is being a "fixer" or problem solver, so whether I have the ability or power to fix or solve an issue I'm facing, I waste time trying my hardest to figure how to do so, determined that at some point surely I'll have a breakthrough and things will go my way. I waste time wishing things were different when I should be walking with my eyes closed in faith, giving God the opportunity to do his work.

Key word here? I. *I* am not God. He is sovereign and capable of handling everything in our lives, if only we will surrender and trust in that sovereignty. That is where peace can bloom.

Worrying will never change anything, but faith, trusting God with everything that weighs on our hearts, and a positive attitude will change everything. We can put our faith in God, believing with full confidence he will take care of the obstacles, guide us around the problems, and carry us through to the end. Or we can choose not to. What a shame that we miss out on a life filled with peace despite our circumstances when it's only a prayer away.

I want to have the type of faith in Christ that will allow me to close my physical eyes and see through the eyes of my heart instead—to believe that God can fight my giants and that the victory has already been won. And that is an attitude worth fighting for.

An Attitude like His

Jesus had every reason to have a bad attitude. In the thirty-three years he walked the earth, he experienced immense hardships, heartaches, and stress. He experienced every emotion imaginable through celebrations, threats, joy, intense grief, overwhelming sorrow, looming disappointments, life interruptions, ridiculous demands, daily pressures, rejection, temptation, hurt, embarrassment, betrayal, and loneliness. So, when we go through really hard times, facing those huge giants that seem to be sucking the life right out of our hearts, we can find solace in knowing that Jesus understands how we feel.

Maybe today you are experiencing one or many of those emotions above. Maybe you feel like nobody understands what you are going through and no one can relate to what you are feeling. Perhaps you have spent so much time living life in a state of stress and anxiety that it's become your norm and you can't even imagine being freed from that self-induced prison and running by faith with peace in your heart, regardless of the storms raging around you or in you. But friend, Jesus understands how you feel, even if it seems like no one else does. And he also holds the key to the peace, freedom, and joy your heart longs for.

In his book *In the Eye of the Storm,* Max Lucado writes:

> When Matthew writes that Jesus had compassion on the people, he is not saying that Jesus felt casual pity for them. No, the term is far more graphic. Matthew is saying that Jesus felt their hurt in his gut:
>
> - He felt the limp of the crippled.
> - He felt the hurt of the diseased.
> - He felt the loneliness of the leper.
> - He felt the embarrassment of the sinful.
>
> And once He felt their hurts, He couldn't help but heal their hurts. He was moved in the stomach by their needs. He was so touched by their needs that He forgot His own needs. He was so moved by the people's hurts that He put His hurts on the back burner.[13]

This brief paragraph from the book beautifully portrays the immense compassion Jesus has for us, as well as his immense understanding of our feelings and our stress.

He understands how we feel not only because he walked the earth as God in human flesh but also because his love for us causes him to actually feel our hurts. He doesn't merely catch our every tear and desire to comfort us; he actually shares our pain, physically and emotionally. But regardless of the disappointments and pain that Jesus suffered in his body on our behalf, what we can hopefully take away from this understanding is the incredible realization that, despite all his sufferings, Jesus never wavered in his attitude.

Jesus never got mad in sin and refused to forgive someone. Jesus never betrayed someone because they had betrayed him. Jesus never turned away from someone in need. Jesus never gossiped about anyone behind their back. Jesus never lacked compassion. Jesus was never selfish. Jesus was never prideful. Jesus was never rebellious or vengeful. Jesus was never unrighteous in his thoughts or actions. Jesus never looked for the bad in anything or anyone. His attitude was not founded on the shifting sand of his earthly circumstances, his earthly surroundings, or his human feelings. It was grounded on the Rock of Salvation, the Father that is bigger than anything he could encounter.

Despite how he was treated, the challenges he faced, the persecution he endured, and the pain he suffered, Jesus's attitude remained one of love, compassion, and optimism. He was able to look past the present to see the future benefits. He knew the truth found in Romans 8:28 that everything serves a higher purpose to glorify God for those who are loved and called by him. Oh, to have an attitude like his.

A few years ago I came across a story about some women shopping in a bookstore. One lady was already browsing the shelves when two other women walked in. One was absolutely stunning—you couldn't help but stare at her. Her features, mannerisms, and elegant clothing looked like they were swiped off the cover of a glamour magazine. Next to this beautiful woman was her friend, who was in a wheelchair. This young woman was somewhat plain looking, slightly overweight, wearing no makeup, and possessed no real sense of style or fashion.

They were an odd pair to be out together, but the lady didn't think much about it and went back to browsing through the bookshelves. A few minutes later, she overheard the pair talking in the next aisle. One was gently and lovingly trying to encourage the other: "It's just your attitude, friend. You can do anything you set your mind to. Life is wonderful; it's all about how we choose to see things. You have so many things to be thankful for. Just try to focus on your blessings instead of burdens. Trust God has everything under control and try not to worry and stress over everything. Life is just too short to live unhappy and anxious all the time."

The bystander didn't mean to eavesdrop, but it was easy to get transfixed on the conversation. The uplifting words and the pleasant, soothing voice of encouragement were so powerful and hope filled, she almost began to believe them herself.

But then the thought crossed her mind about whom those words were coming from. She was surely listening to the words of an obviously beautiful and successful woman who seemed to have it all together and probably didn't have a worry in the world. She sensed a wave of disgruntlement wash in. She began to think, *Well, of course she says all that. She probably has nothing to really worry about. It's easy for her to talk about having a positive attitude and trusting in God when she has everything. Beauty. Money. A perfect body. Health. Gorgeous clothes. Success.* Her attitude after eavesdropping quickly turned from optimism to cynicism.

But when the lady rounded the corner, she stopped dead in her tracks. She saw the two women who had been talking and realized that the encouraging voice, the powerful, positive message overflowing with optimism, had come from the lips of the woman in the wheelchair. The woman who had every right to be mad at God, her circumstances, and the world; to live with a negative attitude over her disability. She surely had plenty to worry and stress about.

Oh, to have an outlook on life like that precious woman in the wheelchair. To have an attitude of hope and a perspective of love, despite having many reasons to have neither. An innate ability and a faith so grounded to intentionally choose to focus on the good things in life, instead of focusing on the negative aspects, and spend every day enjoying the life God has given, no matter what that life looks like. A desire to encourage others to be positive, even when personal circumstances may be negative.

How different our lives are when we have an attitude that allows us to be happy for the blessings of others, even when we are still waiting for our own blessings, and be so grounded in our faith we would never let the adversities of life rob us of a positive attitude.

Developing the type of positive attitude that rules over stress doesn't happen overnight; but with a desire to change, a commitment to practice, persistence, and God's divine intervention, it can and will manifest.

We are provided with grace sufficient to defeat our giants one by one, whether the giant is our circumstances or our attitude about our circumstances, if only we trust God for the victory.

But I Feel Forgotten

As I type those words, I can't help but wonder what you're thinking. Maybe something like, "Well, that sounds great, but you don't know my circumstances. Nobody could have a positive attitude if they were facing the hardships I'm enduring. No one could face these giants and not stress and worry." I understand.

In fact, you may be experiencing a season of life where God seems to be a million miles away and this type of thinking feels absolutely justified. Maybe you're in a season where you are wondering why he is allowing a certain hardship in your life, especially if you have already tried being devoted to loving him, serving him, and trusting his ways, but seemingly to no avail. Maybe no matter how hard you've tried or how desperately you want to be free from stress, your circumstances just won't let up and you can't break loose from the hold anxiety or depression has over you. I imagine that is why you're reading a book about stress, which I applaud you for—because that proves your heart is ready for change. You just need a little pep talk to get you going. That's what I'm here for.

If there is one thing I've learned over many years, which is still hard to accept at times, it's that often God keeps us in a battle rather than immediately answering our prayers for victory in order to take us to a place where we can experience his presence and get some hands-on practice in trusting him and building an attitude like Jesus's. The problem with that is that when we can't see God at work and our prayers feel unheard, our human nature is to feel abandoned and forgotten by God. When those types of thoughts begin to fill our minds, our hearts become riddled with holes that allow for more damaging emotions to seep in—helplessness, rejection, loneliness, and hopelessness.

There have been many occasions when I have had these types of thoughts. As my emotions started playing tricks on my mind, I allowed my anxieties and fears to get the better of me, and I would gradually begin to feel further and further away from God.

In retrospect, I can see how God used those difficult times to help me learn that my responses to situations could teach me a lot about real faith, and that in times of crisis, those responses could either make me or break me. Those situations could make me stronger if I continued to trust God in all his ways, even when I didn't like or understand them. Or they could break me if I turned away from God in anger and frustration, giving the devil a foothold in my heart.

We all experience those feelings of rejection and loneliness at one time or another, whether as a little girl who desperately wishes her daddy would love her, an employee who longs for the acceptance of his or her boss, a mom whose heart aches for a close relationship with her teen, or a woman devastated by her husband leaving her for someone else. There are countless situations that can make us feel rejection, but feeling forgotten or rejected by God can definitely sting the worst.

In Psalm 43, we read about how the psalmist felt rejected and forgotten by God. He writes, "Declare me innocent, O God! Defend me against these ungodly people. Rescue me from these unjust liars. For you are God, my only safe haven. Why have you tossed me aside? Why must I wander around in grief, oppressed by my enemies?" (Ps. 43:1–2). The NIV Bible actually uses the word "rejection" when it says in verse 2, "You are God my stronghold. Why have you rejected me?"

He felt rejected by God. Forgotten. Alone. Weak. Confused. Frustrated. He was at such a low point, he even began questioning God, asking why he was not acting on his behalf and why he was allowing him to suffer. Can you relate? I certainly can. Shall I say, "Been there, done that . . . more than once"? But then, in verses three and four, it seems that the psalmist had some kind of personal revelation, suddenly remembering that God truly was his only help: "Send out your light and your truth; let them guide me. Let them lead me to your holy mountain, to the place where you live. There I will go to the altar of God, to God—the source of all my joy. I will praise you with my harp, O God, my God!"

The psalmist recognized his own weakness and his need for God. He pleaded for God's guidance and intervention in his life and then promised his faithfulness in return. In the midst of his suffering, he chose to willfully and wholeheartedly praise God. He walked in faith, not by sight. In verse 5 we see the psalmist change his attitude completely: "Why am I discouraged? Why is my heart so sad? I will put my hope in God! I will praise him again—my Savior and my God!" I am only guessing here, but it appears he had a personal revelation and recognized that his sour attitude was not helping the situation. He realized that, despite his circumstances, his bad attitude and negative thinking were only making things worse. It's almost like he was telling himself, "Snap out of it!" You could say he implemented the practice of the Three Rs: recognizing how he was thinking, choosing to reject those thoughts, and replacing those thoughts with optimism and trust in God. Instead of continuing to stress and sink further into a pit of anxiety and hopelessness, he called out for the strength to change from the inside out while he endured his circumstances, rather than only asking for God's intervention to change his circumstances.

The psalmist apparently decided to stop listening to that inner voice that had been taunting his self-worth, condemning his self-esteem, and pulling him into a pit of despair and discouragement. He chose to change his attitude; cry out to God for help; and seek guidance, strength, and the will to persevere.

All too often, we find ourselves wrestling with which voice to listen to, but this passage in Psalm 43 is so encouraging and reassures us that we too can overcome stress during our battles of life if we seek out God's face in the midst of it. We can have troubles and still be in God's favor as we allow him to be our strength. We can ask God to change us, even if our circumstances remain the same.

During stressful situations, or just on those hard days when we feel overwhelmed and pulled in every direction, our thoughts can quickly be lured into wondering, *Where is God in all of this?* We wrestle with the thought of being rejected or unseen by God. In the midst of our heartaches, it is easy to listen to the voice of the enemy who wants us to believe that God has left us to face life alone. It is easy to allow our circumstances to divide our hearts, resulting in an inner emotional struggle over whom to believe, what to believe, and whom to turn to. Yet we are reminded in Hebrews 13:5 that God made a promise: "I will never fail you. I will never abandon you." If we believe God's Word is infallible and true, then we must also believe this promise without a shadow of a doubt. Even if we feel abandoned, we indeed are not. When we make our relationship with Christ and his Word a priority on a daily basis, on both carefree days and crazy days, we will be spiritually nourished to fight the battle of the mind, heart, and soul if and when a battle does begin. We will be prepared to preach to ourselves, redirect our thoughts, and change our attitude, just like the psalmist did, which equips us to focus on remembering what we believe and whom we believe in—the Strong One who is always by our side and willing to carry our burdens for us so we can be free of their weight.

Reflection Questions

1. What giants have you been facing that seem too big for God? List them here.

2. How can you begin to trust God to help you face these giants through his strength?

3. Does your stress come from the problems you face or from the way you react to those problems?

4. Are there any changes you can make in your behavior to begin confronting these issues in more productive ways? List some here.

5. Is it possible that you have a bad attitude, which might be contributing to your stress? Explain or reflect on some of the situations where this has happened. This is a difficult question to answer, but be honest with yourself and with God. Meaningful change cannot occur if we are hesitant to confess our own shortcomings and our need for God's help.

6. What areas of your attitude might you need to work on? Look up some Bible verses about attitude, and consider memorizing them to refer to in daily prayer. List some of the verses you selected here:

7. Do you truly believe God is sovereign and capable of handling your problems? Write a brief prayer to God professing your trust in him.

Stress-Busting Scriptures

Therefore do not worry about tomorrow, for tomorrow will worry about itself. Each day has enough trouble of its own.

Matthew 6:34 NIV

❧

I sought the LORD, and he answered me;
he delivered me from all my fears.

Psalm 34:4 NIV

❧

The LORD will guide you always; he will satisfy your needs in a sun-scorched land and will strengthen your frame. You will be like a well-watered garden, like a spring whose waters never fail.

Isaiah 58:11 NIV

❧

Get rid of all bitterness, rage, anger, harsh words, and slander, as well as all types of evil behavior. Instead, be kind to each other, tenderhearted, forgiving one another, just as God through Christ has forgiven you.

Ephesians 4:31–32

❧

And now, dear brothers and sisters, one final thing. Fix your thoughts on what is true, and honorable, and right, and pure, and lovely, and admirable. Think about things that are excellent and worthy of praise.

Philippians 4:8

❧

CHAPTER SEVEN

When Stress Becomes an Addiction

Einstein famously said that the definition of insanity is doing the same thing over and over and expecting different results. Sometimes, however, even when we know we are insanely worried, busy, and stressed—speeding through life without ever stopping to enjoy it while wishing something would change—it is our addiction to adrenaline that compels us to continue the insane behavior.

The world today has become so fast-paced that any deviance from busyness is actually viewed as sinful. When people consider the stereotypes of those who are addicted to adrenaline, successful businessmen and businesswomen come to mind. Executives from all industries have been pulled into the dangerous, chaotic world of never-ending corporate busyness, fueled by a constant rush of dangerous adrenaline.

These people are usually seen typing on their smartphones at every waking moment, working on their laptops in a restaurant when they should be focusing on their family sitting at the table with them, wishing they could have their attention. They run from task to task, thriving on their hurried pace, eating on the go, focused on gaining more and doing more and being more, and feeling as if any deceleration of the speed of their lives would be seen as a negative personal attribute.

They are under the impression they must keep their engine at full throttle at all times, lest they be looked down upon or even left behind. They never cease to multitask. Their identity is dependent on how much they can get done and how quickly they can do it. Some even carry their stress like a badge of honor. When other people acknowledge their busyness or their high level of productivity or success, it recharges their overworked battery and propels them forward, only increasing their addiction and leaving them wanting more.

Then there are the thrill seekers who willingly step into dangerous situations in pursuit of an adrenaline rush, thriving on the emotional high they get from risking their lives in pursuit of adventure. Extreme sports such as parachute jumping, hang gliding, sky diving, mountain climbing, skiing on long steep slopes in mountainous terrain, and bungee jumping bring high risk. Every year, we hear on the news about people involved in these types of high-risk activities, whose lives come to an unfortunate end. Even though there is a high level of inherent danger in many extreme sports, people still participate in them because of their addiction to adrenaline.

But people in the corporate world and extreme thrill seekers are not the only ones who thrive on or get addicted to adrenaline—whether purposely or inadvertently. This addiction is present in your everyday average human being who thinks they are just living the normal life—for example, those whose busyness never ends, such as stay-at-home parents. They spend every waking moment changing diapers, cleaning the house, fixing meals, buying groceries, sewing on buttons, administering medicine, driving to playdates, coaching cheerleading squads or sports teams, helping with community service projects, caring for sick family members, serving on church committees, mowing the lawn, planting flowers, and paying bills. The ones who fall into the category of "no rest for the weary."

And what about all the hardworking citizens who work tirelessly to support their families or even work multiple jobs to stay afloat? Consider the lives of third-shift employees who spend all night working and then all day tending to the family obligations mentioned previously. People from every walk of life can have adrenaline pumping through their veins at dangerous levels for extended periods of time, like a poison they don't even know they consumed, all while putting their lives in jeopardy by living amid the toxicity of chronic stress.

Just as a race car is fueled by gasoline, our bodies are fueled by the natural hormone drug produced when we are under stress—epinephrine (a.k.a. adrenaline). Epinephrine, along with other hormones like cortisol, is released when our bodies are faced with either excitement or stress.

Epinephrine can be good when someone is faced with a life-threatening crisis, such as needing superhuman strength to lift a wrecked car off of a person trapped underneath. But when this hormone constantly secretes into our bodies because of unrelenting stress, it can be extremely harmful to our health.

Having a rush of stress hormones surge through our bodies for a brief time period, like when we are under immediate distress or in a crisis, is the way God created our bodies to cope and deal with stressful situations. But when those hormones are activated over a long period of time and our bodies are overexposed to all the stress hormones, our entire body and functions can be negatively impacted. Living with chronic stress causes so many physical problems, but unfortunately, they often go unrecognized as being related to stress and sometimes are even diagnosed as other diseases. For example, symptoms such as anxiety, depression, digestive problems, headaches, heart disease, heart attacks, sleep problems, weight gain, memory problems, and concentration impairments are just some of the problems toxic stress can cause, according to studies by the Mayo Clinic on how chronic stress puts your health at risk. It can even lead to Alzheimer's and eventually prove fatal.[14]

An addiction to adrenaline is often difficult to diagnose because it pushes us beyond what is healthy, yet falls under the guise of what we have come to believe is just normal life. People who are addicted may find that they make sure they are doing something . . . all the time. There is never room for downtime because that would mean they are not needed or may feel unproductive. The rush they receive from busyness keeps them going from day to day; they relish in compliments and pats on the back received from others, whether for securing a profitable deal with a client, planning a successful women's ministry event at church, or being the best PTA mom of all time. Their minds are fueled by the praise, and they can't even fathom taking a day of rest.

On the flip side, some people thrive on an insane addiction to adrenaline simply as an attempt to keep their focus on anything that distracts them from the pain and heartbreak of their past or the stressful adversities in their present. They keep busy to prevent themselves from thinking about the burdens on their heart or the problems in their life. They keep busy in order to avoid dealing with relationships. But, eventually, the outcome is the same and their adrenaline gives them a rush they can no longer live without, and it may become impossible to just sit still or slow down.

No matter what the root cause of adrenaline addiction may be, adrenaline junkies are always overwhelmed, pulled in every direction (often by choice), and stressed to the max. They thrive on the need to feel necessary and productive and possess an insatiable sense of urgency and need for accomplishment. If anything comes up that derails their well-laid-out plans, sheer panic could potentially set in.

Whether you thrive on an addiction to adrenaline on purpose or the lifestyle you lead is simply laced with stress due to pressures and obligations, an addiction to stress and adrenaline can be as hard to break as any other addiction that threatens to steal or end a life.

There Is Always Hope for Change

Regardless of what category you fall into, there is always hope for change. Often the biggest problem faced by adrenaline junkies is admitting they actually are addicted, and the biggest problem faced by people whose stress leads to great anxiety and physical health issues is admitting that change is necessary—not only for the sake of our own mental and physical health, but for our marriages, children, families, friendships, work relationships, and overall lives.

When we live in a constant state of stress, adrenaline dangerously coursing through our veins without ceasing, there is no way our heath won't eventually be affected. Just as any illness left ignored and untreated will worsen, the damage of stress is the same. If you have deceived yourself to believe that stress isn't a problem for you, and you can handle the busyness of life without skipping a beat or suffering any consequences, are you beginning to second-guess yourself after reading all this information? My prayer is your answer is a confident "Yes." Stress is rampant in our society, so to think that any person is immune to it, or can handle it with ease, is painfully unrealistic.

But there is hope. The sooner we recognize we have been inadvertently pulled into a lifestyle of incredible busyness, chaos, and overcommitment, or even if we allowed ourselves to step into a life of stress, the sooner we can begin to reach for healing. We can stare our reality in the face rather than turn a blind eye and work toward purposely trying to prevent all of these physical, mental, emotional, and spiritual problems from occurring.

Becoming aware that we need a stress intervention is the first step. Seeking Jesus as the answer is the second.

A Step toward Healing

I once heard an old cliché that said, if the devil can't hinder our relationship with God by making us immoral, he'll simply make us busy. If we take a good hard look around, there are a lot of godly people who are too busy for Jesus. Let's face it, if we are too busy to spend time with God, then we are absolutely way too busy! Just as spending too little time with our family and loved ones results in damaged relationships, spending too little time with Jesus can damage our relationship with him.

The Bible tells us that one day we will all stand in front of God, accountable for our actions, which includes being held accountable for how we spent our time and what kept us busy all of our lives. "For we must all stand before Christ to be judged. We will each receive whatever we deserve for the good or evil we have done in this earthly body" (2 Cor. 5:10).

Knowing that one day we will have to account for our lives should compel us to ask ourselves the hard questions: What is keeping me most busy? Where do I devote the majority of my time? What calls for my attention most often? What am I neglecting? What should I let go of? Is my time well spent? Will I be proud to talk with God about how I spent most of my time on earth?

In many cases, our answers to these first questions may be primarily from the categories of work or family. These are important aspects of life that are necessary to spend our time on, and God calls us to be diligent and devoted to both. However, when we allow even the good things of life to deter us from our spiritual lives, causing us to lose sight of what our priorities are and pushing us into a lifestyle of long-term chronic stress, changes are necessary.

John 9:4 says, "We must quickly carry out the tasks assigned us by the one who sent us. The night is coming, and then no one can work." Here we see Jesus telling his disciples that they were to be busy with God's business. Not just busy with impressive acts of service but busy using their time wisely and in big and small ways in their everyday lives that would glorify God. Psalm 39:5–7 says, "You have made my life no longer than the width of my hand. My entire lifetime is just a moment to you; at best, each of us is but a breath. We are merely moving shadows, and all our busy rushing ends in nothing. We heap up wealth, not knowing who will spend it. And so, Lord, where do I put my hope? My only hope is in you."

When David wrote the psalm above, he was acknowledging that life is short and that we should therefore focus our time on the types of busyness, and business, that really matter. He realized that going through life apart from God is meaningless and that his only hope for real happiness, peace, and joy is in God.

How God's heart longs for us to embrace the desire to be rescued by his hope, just like David did.

The Rescuer

One sunny spring day when my daughter Kaitlyn was only eighteen months old, my family and I had driven over to my mother's house for a quick visit. While we were there, she mentioned there was a family heirloom she wanted to give to me, but it was stored away in the attic. I instructed my then four-year-old daughter, Morgan, to stay downstairs with her daddy while I went with my mother to the attic. I proceeded up to the second floor of the house, holding Kaitlyn in my arms.

As I was searching for the box in the attic, Kaitlyn was toddling around the cramped room, curiously checking out the strange surroundings, while looking extremely cute and inquisitive, as little girls do. As I began searching in one particular area of the attic, Kaitlyn pattered across the bare wooden floor in her new, white walking shoes, wandering just a few feet away. Just as I looked up to call her back toward me, she vanished from sight. In a split second, she was gone.

As it turned out, there was a hole in the attic floor, which my mother was not even aware existed—a hole just big enough for a baby to fall straight through with ease.

For the first time in my entire life, I involuntarily screamed in sheer horror. I could not stop screaming. My heart stopped as fear filled every bone in my body. It was as if time stood still. My legs felt as heavy as lead as I tried to frantically rush to the exact spot where she had been standing just one second earlier. It was then that I saw the gaping hole for the very first time. As I glared down the hole where my baby once stood, my eyes caught a glimpse of her as she plummeted downward, just before she impacted with the ground, eyes locked on her falling in horror as I stood there helplessly, above. My mind could not grasp the reality that my baby was potentially plunging to her death on the hard concrete garage floor twenty feet below.

But when her fall came to an abrupt halt, I witnessed something I can hardly explain. A miracle. A rescue, above all rescues that I had ever or would ever be blessed to see. It happened in a millisecond. I watched as her tiny little body collided with the ground and bounced off the hard concrete floor . . . like a soft rubber ball. It was as if she had landed on a fluffy pillow of cotton, or even a tiny trampoline, and just gingerly bounced off. My mind raced with confusion, but in that moment, the numbing fear that had overtaken my body left me no mental capacities to try to process what I thought I had seen.

With all this happening in less than a few seconds, I continued to scream and tears began to hinder my vision. As soon as I saw her impact, I flew down the stairwell at the speed of lighting, panicked and unable to breathe, taking three and four steps at a time, my mother right at my heels. This was definitely an example of the fight or flight syndrome taking place. The stress hormones raced through my body like wildfire, giving me the speed and strength to bolt down a flight of stairs like lightning, only touching a few steps along the way.

I ran through the house, flung open the garage door, and saw my precious baby laying there motionless on the floor. I gently scooped her up in my arms. I have never heard a sound so precious as the sound of her cries in that moment. But sheer terror set in as I imagined the internal damage that had surely been incurred by her fall. I wondered if her skull or any other tiny bones were cracked or shattered, although I could not see any damage with the naked eye.

My then husband, who had still been sitting downstairs with my other daughter, was absolutely terror stricken, having no idea what all the sudden commotion was about. When he finally found me sobbing hysterically in the garage, holding our wailing little girl, the blood drained from his face as the reality of what had occurred sunk into his brain. We immediately dashed to the car and rushed to the emergency room as thoughts of the worst filled our hearts and minds and our hearts raced at unhealthy levels.

Strangely, by the time we arrived at the hospital twenty minutes later, Kaitlyn's tears had dried and she was acting like her normal, cute little self. My husband and I exchanged worried glances as we sat in the ER waiting room for what seemed like an eternity. With each strained breath I took, my worry increased. *Why wasn't she crying? Was she in shock? Did she have a concussion? Did she have brain damage? Was she bleeding internally? Or worse? Oh God, please see my little girl. Please let her be okay.* I hadn't really had time to process what I had seen happen in the garage. I just needed to know my baby was going to live.

When we finally saw the doctor and explained what had happened, a perplexing look washed across his face. Instead of ordering MRIs and X-rays, he was unsuccessfully trying to keep Kaitlyn from grabbing the stethoscope around his neck. As he gently tried to examine her little body, she giggled with delight.

He could find no injuries, other than a small egg-shaped bump on one side of her forehead. There was no external or internal bleeding, and she did not have a scratch, bruise, concussion, or broken bone in her little fragile body. The doctor told us that had I not told him I witnessed the fall, he would seriously doubt whether or not it actually happened.

Kaitlyn was completely unharmed. She was the same little girl as when she had woken up that morning. But I was not the same. In fact, I was changed forever. Do you think it was luck that my baby was unharmed after such a horrific incident? Absolutely not. I walked out of the ER with renewed faith and thankfulness for the sovereign God in my life, who can perform miracles we cannot explain or comprehend—a life-giving gratitude that he was not only my baby's Rescuer that day, but the Rescuer of the whole world.

I believe with my whole heart that God rescued my baby from a fall that should have taken her life. My only explanation for what I saw is that an angel was sent to her rescue in that very moment and caught my precious child in the safety of her soft, white as snow, beautiful wings. Or maybe God himself stepped in and leaned down from his throne in his most perfect and precise timing, catching Kaitlyn securely in the palm of his loving, mighty hands.

Either way, Psalm 91:4 took on a whole new meaning for me that day. "He will cover you with his feathers. He will shelter you with his wings. His faithful promises are your armor and protection." My child found protection, safety, and life in the wings of God. He faithfully rescued and protected one of his children, who just happened to also be one of mine. But this rescue was not only for my baby; it was for me. I was speechless at the favor God had bestowed upon my child, and I vowed to never doubt the vastness of God's love for me again. The miracle that happened in this situation is beyond our human capacity to grasp, but there is simply no other explanation than God's hand at work.

Sweet friend, do you need to be rescued today? Do you feel like your life is spiraling out of control, consumed with stress, worry, and busyness? Do you feel like you are plummeting downward, wondering how hard your impact will be when you finally get to the point of hitting rock bottom or reaching your breaking point? Do you need someone to put your hope in because the situations in your life seem hopeless and change seems impossible? Have you been living off the rush of adrenaline, addicted to its power over your heart and your life?

Remember this . . . God is not only capable of rescuing us from physical harm, but also from emotional and mental harm, as well. He longs to be our rescuer, even when we are blinded to the fact that we need to be rescued. His peace is the rescue we need when we are trapped in a life of toxic stress, and it is available if we ask for it and want it bad enough to change.

In 2 Samuel 22, David sings a song of praise to the Lord for delivering him from his enemies. I find it interesting, however, that before the Lord acted, David had to ask to be rescued: "But in my distress I cried out to the LORD; yes, I cried to my God for help. He heard me from his sanctuary; my cry reached his ears" (v. 7). Then we see that David thanks God for his rescue in verse 33: "It is God who arms me with strength and makes my way perfect" (NIV).

David faced more adversity than we would want to shake a stick at, but he remained strong in his faith by relying on a holy strength that he could not muster on his own. He didn't choose a slingshot as his weapon; he chose God.

Sometimes we may feel like we are running a close second to David in the race for the worst adversity. But just as it was for David, strength and rescue are available to each one of us. All we have to do is ask and believe God will work on our behalf and give us what we need to overcome and rise above the adversities, problems, obligations, and stress we are facing. When we seek his deliverance, like David did, God first gives us the strength to persevere, then he provides the rescue.

If you are willing to admit stress has become a problem in your life and that just maybe you are even an addict, then take a moment right now and ask God to rescue you and replace your stress with the gift of peace he so freely offers. Believe with your whole heart he hears your prayers and will do exactly that. Envision his mighty hand stretching down from the heavens, ready to catch you and deliver you from the toxin of stress.

In God's Strength

If you just paused and prayed, asking God to rescue your heart from whatever has been holding your joy and peace captive, then I rejoice with you! Today is the first day of the rest of your new life, filled with peace instead of stress. If you have admitted to yourself you just might be an adrenaline junkie—living a life overloaded with stress and busyness, filled with an overflow of emotions that are increasingly taking a toll on your mind, body, and soul—then let today be the first day of your "new normal."

Change is often hard, awkward, and uncomfortable. When it comes to saving your life, however, change can become mandatory. But thanks to Jesus, we do not have to strive for change in our own strength (or lack of strength).

Many years ago, my stepmother was diagnosed with cancer. She went through all the necessary treatments, and we were thrilled beyond belief when her doctor announced the good news of her remission. Unfortunately, a year later her cancer returned. Although she went through the standard rounds of chemotherapy and radiation treatments once again, her body was not responding and the cancer continued to spread. After a long and fiercely fought battle, her tenure on earth was drawing to a close. My family and I arranged to make the four-hour trip to go and visit her, knowing it might possibly be for the last time.

I walked into her hospital room and found her lying in the bed looking so weak and frail, helpless to beat the disease that had waged war on her body. I fought back the tears as I struggled with feelings of helplessness. My deepest sorrow came bubbling up to the surface as I tried with all my might to fight back the tears. I found myself wanting to do something for her, anything . . . but there was nothing I could do except wish to the depths of my soul that I could infuse her with the strength she needed to carry on. But I felt weak and had no strength to give, and even if I did, my strength held no power.

Unfortunately, less than two years ago, I went through the same exact experience with my father. He had survived throat cancer and was suffering from COPD due to smoking for many years. He had also survived lung cancer, but then his cancer returned. His initial treatments went well, but eventually, as all too often is the case, the cancer began to win the battle. Again, I found myself sitting by his hospital bed in a hospice center for an entire week. The first few days, he was alert, laughing, talking, and seemed like himself. I was sure that he would go home soon and that there had been a mistake in his diagnosis.

But a couple of days later, when only my dad and I were in the room at the time, the doctor arrived and pulled up a chair beside his bed to chat. They made small talk for a few minutes, he made a few jokes and it seemed the conversation was going fine, until she put on her serious face and got down to business. She shared with little emotion what the future held and told my dad he would never be going home—that within a few days, he would die. My dad just looked at her blankly and nodded his head and said "Okay," and she continued to talk us through how things would progress over the next few days.

I sat there in silence, stunned at her words, appalled by her bluntness and seemingly uncaring bedside manner. My face felt numb. Crocodile tears threatened to burst forth but I tried with all

my might to hold them back and not fall apart. Inside I was screaming, but on the outside, there was only silence. My mind was void
of any words that I could possibly say when she went to leave the
room. My heart so broken for my dad, and fear filled every ounce
of my being at the thought of watching someone I loved take their
last breath. Fear for how he was surely feeling hearing those words
that his life would soon be over. Again, I was rendered helpless,
hopeless, and without any strength or ability to do anything to
make things okay again.

It had been bad enough seeing my stepmother pass away, but at
least she wasn't as aware and cogniznant of her impending departure from this earth. My dad was as clear minded and normal and
jovial as he'd ever been, and he knew. It was almost more than I
could handle, and I wanted to climb up in the bed with him, but
felt I needed to be strong for him and not fall apart. The weight of
the emotions and my swirling thoughts were similar to the ones
I had felt when I saw my stepmother for the last time, and I was
reminded of what brought me a little comfort back then.

The day I left the hospital after saying goodbye to my stepmother
for the last time, I had returned home with a heavy heart and had
looked to God's Word for comfort. I remembered coming across
two verses that seeped deep into the cracks of my heart, which
desperately needed to be filled with God's love in place of sadness:
"Therefore, be careful to obey every command I am giving you today,
so you may have strength to go in and take over the land you are
about to enter. If you obey, you will enjoy a long life in the land the
Lord swore to give your ancestors and to you, their descendants—a
land flowing with milk and honey!" (Deut. 11:8–9).

At first glance, this passage may not seem even remotely rele-
vant to what I was going through at the time, but God had a special
message in mind for me. In this passage, the Lord is telling the
Israelites about their soon-to-be entrance into the Promised Land.
He had been reminding them of all the miracles and amazing things

that had happened during their journey. He knew, based on their history of sinful actions and attitudes, that they were easily tempted by idols, which had caused them to lose their focus on God and be devoid of strength.

In these verses, we find the Lord warning the Israelites about losing sight of their priorities, reminding them the only place they will find strength is in him. The Lord also wanted them to understand their strength could not come from merely carrying out rituals or sacrifices in his honor—strength would only come from full obedience. In fact, in Deuteronomy 11:18 the Lord says, "So commit yourselves wholeheartedly to these words of mine. Tie them to your hands and wear them on your forehead as reminders."

Their strength could only come from wholehearted obedience to all of the Lord's commands. They were to even wear his words on their hands and foreheads so they would never forget them. And even today—in our society of rampant busyness, unrelenting stress, and adrenaline addictions—God wants us to do the same. His desire is that we come to understand the importance of walking with him every day, because that is where we gain our strength and our peace.

As I sat vigil beside my dad's bedside, watching him take his very last breath on earth and leave this world to go be with Jesus, again I had to depend on the strength of God—because I had none of my own. I was emotionally and physically drained and exhausted. I recalled these verses, reminding me where strength would come from in the coming days and weeks as we mourned the loss and I intentionally sought out God's peace as well.

In painful situations such as losing those we love or other heartbreaking circumstances, it feels more natural to call on God for strength and peace. But during the chaos of everyday life, we tend to forget we need it then as well. If you are trying to be strong and run through life like a freight train based solely on your own strength, skills, or knowledge, then stress is the only possible outcome. You do not have the power within to maintain the strength needed to persevere, and you will soon find that real rest, relief, relaxation, and peace seem unattainable.

God instructs us to obey in the big things, of course, but also in our small, seemingly insignificant daily thoughts and actions. This obedience infuses us with a spiritual strength that equips us to handle those tough situations that are far beyond our human level of strength to handle, regardless of whether we are in the hospital bed or standing beside it.

This daily obedience is where we find the infusion of emotional strength that allows us to walk in his peace when we face doubts and fears. Strength to walk in his joy when we cannot find any reason to be joyful. Strength to stand firm in our faith when things seem hopeless. And strength to be strong when the painful things of life are taking their toll on our hearts.

Most importantly, our desire to walk with God on a daily basis gives us the strength to not only acknowledge when changes need to be made in our lives but to believe he will provide the strength and the wisdom to decipher which changes we need to make.

Each day when we get out of bed, we have a choice to make about where our strength will come from to face the day ahead. Will we rely on ourselves or will we rely on God? Will we try to rely on our human strength to persevere or will we seek the strength God provides to our spirits, enabling us to get through even the most painful of days? Will we continue to assume that if we try hard enough we will have the power to change or make changes happen, or will we realize that God, and God alone, possesses the power to do so? Will we continue to let stress rob us of enjoying life, or will we slow down long enough to ask God to fill us with peace so we can enjoy life as he intended?

If your life is stressful, chaotic, busy, and overloaded, then I imagine your heart is tired and your body is weak. Maybe you feel like you are dangling over a pit, dangerously close to the end of your rope. Maybe you feel as I did, standing by my stepmother's hospital bed, aching for the power to make things better, while feeling weighed down by the heavy burden of my helplessness.

Maybe you want to be strong, but you have no strength left to lift life's weights from your heart. If so, maybe now you realize that stress has taken its toll and you are finally ready to change and be changed.

Take comfort in reading Matthew 11:28–29: "Then Jesus said, 'Come to me, all of you who are weary and carry heavy burdens, and I will give you rest. Take my yoke upon you. Let me teach you, because I am humble and gentle at heart, and you will find rest for your souls.'"

Do you see the sweet promise? Not only for rest but for peace in your heart? Are you ready to spend some time in God's presence, soaking in these Scriptures and letting him teach you how to make the promises in his Word a reality in your life? Are you ready to feel a holy and empowered strength in your weakened spirit?

My prayer is that the Lord is slowly using this book to open your eyes and help you see, maybe for the very first time, the damage that your addiction to adrenaline, busyness, and/or stress may be having on you, your heart, your health, your faith, and your family. My hope is that you can sense Jesus reaching deep into the places of your spirit that nothing else has been able to reach and planting the seed for a compelling desire to change and be changed.

Psalm 38:9 says, "You know what I long for, Lord; you hear my every sigh." God already knows the longings of your heart. Take a moment and talk to him about them, remembering that when you ask, you will receive.

⟲ Reflection Questions

1. Consider any situations or circumstances that have been causing you great stress. Think of your most stressful circumstance
right now and write it in the space below, and then answer the
questions that follow. Use these questions as a thought-provoking
activity for additional stressful situations you are facing as well.

A stressful situation or circumstance:

_____

_____

_____

Ways you have dealt with this situation in the past:

_____

_____

_____

Do you always hope for different results, even if you are continually addressing the problem in the same manner?

_____

_____

_____

Ways to approach this problem differently:

_____

_____

_____

Benefits that may result from changing your reaction and/or
action toward the issue:

_____

_____

_____

Consequences of continuing in the same old ways that have not worked in the past:

_____

_____

_____

If you have been addressing the above issues in the same ways over and over again, while expecting or hoping for different results, pray for guidance on how to begin making different choices and asking God to give you the strength to change and the humility to rely on his power alone.

2. Is it possible that you are an adrenaline junkie? What category do you see yourself in: the Accomplisher, the Personal Deflector, the Deflector, or the Dramatist? If you are aware of some areas within yourself that you need to change, what actions can you take to make strides for personal improvement in those areas of weakness?

3. Are you too busy for your own good? What responsibilities do you currently hold that you can delegate to someone else to relieve some of the pressure you feel? If you are unsure, spend some time in prayer, asking for clarity about God's priorities for your life, or write your prayer below. Seek his will about what things you should be devoting your time to, and what you should let go of.

4. Have you ever asked God to rescue your heart and refresh your spirit? If not, what has prevented you from doing that?

5. If you have asked God for "rescue" in the past, and he intervened in your life in divine ways, jot down your memories of that experience. Tuck these memories into your heart and allow them to be your motivation to turn your life and all your current stressors over to him today.

6. If you have never recognized the need to be rescued but now understand the power of God's intervention, write a personal prayer of humility and praise to God; express your need to be rescued, while committing to trust him with the situations in your life and asking for his power and strength to persevere.

7. Has there been a time when you knew that God's strength was the only reason you were able to make it through a serious adversity? How does knowing he is capable of holding you up equip you to face the issues you are facing today?

Stress-Busting Scriptures

Those who know your name will trust in you, for you,
LORD, have never forsaken those who seek you.

Psalm 9:10 NIV

In you our fathers put their trust; they trusted and you
delivered them. They cried to you and were saved;
in you they trusted and were not disappointed.

Psalm 22:4–5 NIV

Be very careful, then, how you live—not as unwise but as wise,
making the most of every opportunity, because the days are evil.
Therefore do not be foolish, but understand what the Lord's will is.

Ephesians 5:15–17 NIV

Give justice to the poor and the orphan; uphold the rights of the
oppressed and the destitute. Rescue the poor and helpless;
deliver them from the grasp of evil people.

Psalm 82:3–4

And this world is fading away, along with everything that people
crave. But anyone who does what pleases God will live forever.

1 John 2:17

CHAPTER EIGHT

Choose Your Weapons Wisely

People deal with stress in many different ways. Some people work off their stress by participating in sports or exercise, while others want to relax in a hot tub or sit in a sauna. Some take a relaxing vacation, while others snuggle up with a good book. But, unfortunately, far too many people turn to dangerous and even deadly choices in their desperate search for stress relief.

Many people turn to alcohol, caffeine, food, cigarettes, and illegal or prescription drugs when they find it impossible to find stress relief in any other way. It breaks my heart to see people so desperate for relief they will do anything for it—especially when all they really need is Jesus.

Regrettably, some people honestly believe they can deal with their stress better if they have a few drinks every night to "take the edge off." Enjoying an alcoholic drink in the evenings has become a favorite pastime in our society, but when it becomes a necessity to deal with life, it becomes a threat to our health. Other people feel eating will ease their stress and make them feel more relaxed, so they become consumed with filling themselves with food, hoping the comfort of food will soothe the emptiness they feel. Many others turn to drugs to help them either cope or forget, while convincing themselves their drug use is only "until things get better." But just like every lie the devil throws at us, succumbing to these falsehoods will only lead to more stress.

None of these methods bring permanent relief; most times, they'll only exacerbate the problem. If people constantly seek out stress relief in all the wrong places and end up making one bad choice after another, trying to Band-Aid the problem rather than unearth the root of the problem and deal with it, addictions in many forms can secretly begin to rear their ugly heads—which eventually brings on more stress and anxiety than they ever thought possible. The consequences of the addiction only compound all the stressors that were already present. Sadly, for people who have kicked their former habits of substance abuse or any harmful addictive behaviors, stress is one of the major factors known to cause a relapse, even after prolonged periods of abstinence.

In this day and age, there are so many worldly weapons available at our fingertips. Typically, these are the first things we reach for to help us win the war against stress. And while these "weapons" might seem more enticing and perhaps more fun than turning to God—things like massages, vacations, pedicures, shopping, wine, eating, and the like—they only bring temporary comfort and are completely inadequate for fighting the battles that life brings. The fleeting weapons of this world will always fail to protect us when (not if, but when) the next stressful situation rages in. When charging toward the giant of stress in our lives, we must choose our weapons for the battle very carefully.

Choose God

Wouldn't it be awesome if we could ask God for strength and immediately feel a physical, electrical infusion of spirituality, becoming instantly empowered with new energy and unshakable faith to face the days ahead? Maybe even transform into a superhero with superhuman strength in the blink of an eye? If God willed that to happen, it certainly would be incredible, but he usually chooses more subtle ways to intervene in our lives so we can discover where true strength for the battle really comes from.

Real strength results from persistent communication and fellowship with him and allowing his words to guide us through each day. Just as David beat Goliath because he chose God as his weapon, we can choose God as our weapon of choice when facing battles of any kind.

Isaiah 40:31 says, "But those who trust in the LORD will find new strength. They will soar high on wings like eagles. They will run and not grow weary. They will walk and not faint." Fully trusting in the Lord is where we draw the kind of strength we need—that spiritual infusion of power which comes from daily devotion to biblical principles. It is this constant connection with God that enables us to be transformed and empowered by him. How can we continue to feel stressed if we are transformed and empowered in Christ? If we have a peace that surpasses all understanding fully present in our hearts, how likely are we cower to stress the first time something else stressful comes up? Think about it.

So what does spiritual strength actually look like? In our ego-centric society, we typically consider strength to be a physical attribute characterized by bulging muscles and a toned body. Movies of today reinforce this mindset, constantly portraying humans with inhuman strength as the only ones who have the power to initiate change, impact lives, or do good deeds. But, in God's opinion, this is an extremely distorted view.

Let's imagine God had a camera and began taking pictures of people who were pillars of strength in his eyes. What types of snapshots do you think he would take? I can imagine him capturing a shot of a mother on her knees every morning, pouring out her heart and pleading for him to protect her children as they grow up in our broken society.

I envision seeing God taking a picture of a man in a high-rise office building going against corporate political correctness to stand up for ethics and integrity, despite whether or not negative consequences to his career may follow.

Picture God photographing a pastor in the pulpit, or on a street corner, encouraging anyone within earshot to embrace God's grace and love; a family staring at the smoldering remnants of their home, trusting God will provide for them in the coming days; a teenager deciding to not give in to peer pressure because he made a vow of purity to God; a couple trying to forgive each other, just as Christ forgave them, as they work through the difficulties in their marriage; a husband fighting his temptation to view pornography by spending time in God's Word and asking God for the willpower to control lustful desires; a divorced woman surrendering her anger and bitterness toward her exhusband, while rediscovering a peace and joy that had escaped her heart; or a man who loves his family so much he works three jobs without resentment, thanking God for these opportunities to provide for those he loves.

I can only imagine God would have a phenomenal heavenly photo album packed with pictures—beautiful pictures of infinite scores of his children who are exhibiting spiritual strength during the most trying times, with each and every one making him one very proud Daddy.

Ask yourself this question: If God really did have a camera, would he consider you picture-worthy, as someone who finds strength in him? If your answer is no, then that's okay. If we're being completely and brutally honest, I wonder if any of us would admit that we feel strong and empowered. Even people who seem to be a pillar of confidence and strength may feel weak and defeated on the inside due to the constant demands of the stresses of life and endless problems or responsibilities.

Regardless of which category we see ourselves in, we can always make a commitment to more intentionally lean into our faith and choose God as our source of stress relief over anything else. We can ask God to help us gain strength to think differently and live differently, one little step at a time.

Let's look at a few examples of how to do this. One method is to simply start carving out some time each day, or even one day a week, to create a sense of quiet, stillness, or peace. Spend time meditating, praying, or just letting your mind rest. Ask God to help you stop trying to control things that are clearly out of your control—this alone will help minimize your stress. When something bad happens, retrain your mind to start thinking about things in a different way with a different perspective. Don't just immediately throw your hands up in the air and exclaim, "Why me?" or "Not again!" or "Why can't I ever have a moment's peace?!" Instead, ask yourself how you can handle the situation at hand differently than you have in the past and how you would feel and act if you did. How might changing your perspective and reaction affect your stress level? Rather than keeping all your thoughts and emotions bottled up, like a carbonated drink being shaken up just waiting to explode at the first hint of the cap being loosened, write everything down in a journal and just "brain dump" anything that comes to mind. Let that be an outlet where you can say anything you want, knowing there are no repercussions but allowing yourself to be freed from the toxicity of the stress of those pent-up emotions.

When we clear our hearts and minds of stress and begin to transform ourselves from the inside out, we prepare ourselves to be more open to God. Our eyes can see him better, our spirits long for him more, and the desire for peace and inner spiritual strength begins to take precedence over the temptation to let anxiety rule.

Choose God's Word

I found myself in a dark field in the middle of the night, yet I was not alone. Although I could sense the presence of other people scattered throughout the field, I could not see them clearly because the only light was coming from a few slivers of moonbeams that crept across the acres. When I looked up, I saw a figure hovering near me. My eyes strained to try to make sense of what I was seeing.

This figure, along with all the others roaming throughout the barren field, seemed to be the silhouette of a soldier exuding the odorless scent of control and power. Suddenly, deep in my soul, I felt an overwhelming sense of danger so thick it was as if I could reach out and touch it, although I had no idea what danger lurked in this unknown place.

Before I could comprehend what was going on, I was thrown to the ground with great force, landing hard on my back as my head hit the cold dirt. I felt the weight of one of the figures pinning me firmly to the ground with my arms pulled tightly across my chest, prohibiting me from fighting back or trying to defend myself.

I could feel the hatred spewing from its spirit and the presence of evil dripping from the empty face. As I heard the wails of the other people in the field, my mind was overcome with fear and confusion about what was happening. Then, in the midst of this heart-ripping struggle, I had a divine revelation, as if God's voice were echoing through the meadows, but only I could hear him.

I became acutely aware to the depths of my soul that God's Word was my only hope. Scripture was my only lifeline. His promises would protect me. His words held power over evil. I knew his sovereignty was my only chance in this battle against unseen forces.

As could only happen in the context of a dream, where anything is possible, my body instantly shrunk down to the size of a pencil. I wriggled out of this evil being's grip and flung myself onto the pages of an open Bible, which just happened to be lying in the tall grasses beside me.

I immediately reached over with both hands and grabbed a handful of pages by the corner. I began to roll with all my might, tearing the pages from the creases of the book, and wrapping myself tightly into the pages of God's Word, as if I were a caterpillar entombing itself in a cocoon.

Instantly, the faceless enemies retreated in fear. My spirit felt the evil leap from my presence, and I was freed from its weight upon me. Then, as if nothing had occurred, all was quiet. My heart was beating quickly and my breathing was labored. Although I was shaken up and dismayed, I was left unharmed.

And then I awoke from the deep slumber that had been holding me captive in this nightmare and tried to wrap my mind around the very real war I had just been engaged in.

As I lay there, staring with blurry, tear-filled eyes into the pitch-black darkness of 3:00 a.m., my mind raced in every direction. My thoughts stumbled over each other, each one trying to be the first to figure out what had just happened. Although I knew I was safe and sound in my own warm bed, my husband sleeping quietly beside me, my heart felt ravaged by the battle between good and evil that I had just encountered in the deepest recesses of my mind.

In that fragile moment with God, as my nightmare still hung in the quietness of the air, I could do nothing else but pray. I spent the next hour in deep conversation with Jesus, and my spirit was awakened to what this dream really meant. I don't claim to be a dream interpreter, but I knew this was a message from God.

It suddenly became crystal clear that my entire family and I had been engaged in a fierce battle of spiritual warfare. You see, the past year had been filled with one blow after another, piling stress upon stress upon more stress, but I had merely attributed it all to life and human mistakes instead of giving credit where credit was due. Credit the enemy would gladly accept.

The devil loves to cause trouble, which is evidenced by the troubles that he brought upon Job in the Bible. Job was a good man who trusted God. And although God did not cause Job's troubles, he did allow the devil to, which ultimately proved Job's trust and devotion to God in spite of overwhelming adversity and loss. I certainly don't know whether God caused our troubles to teach us valuable lessons of which we are still learning or whether he allowed the devil to cause them to test the faith and devotion of our family. But, either way, I had been feeling a little like Job might have felt. My losses seemed huge, my emotions were raw, and my heart had been hurting. I had been so focused on *why* we were suffering through all these adversities that I had neglected to think about *who* could get me through them or *how* God was going to mold our hardships to be for his glory.

So, in the middle of the night, when the house was silent and it was just me and my sweet Jesus, all the fears and hurts and longings of my heart overflowed onto his feet like never before. My thoughts poured out of my mind like rapid waters rushing over the rocks of a swollen river. Amid my pleas for mercy, compassion, and protection, I felt a sense of freedom drench my spirit.

It was a strange sensation—a lightness and a release, neither of which I had felt in a very long time. It was a peace that had been eluding me for months as my mind struggled with negative emotions and the stressful situations that had kept my heart in bondage. As I allowed my mind to be engulfed with God's love, I was overcome with gratefulness, and I felt compelled to ask him . . . why? Yet, this time, it was a different *why*. Why would he care so much about me? Why did I matter? Why would he go to such lengths to get my attention and to rescue me from this invisible battle? Why did he die for me? Why does he love his children so much? Why was I worth it?

The only answer is a love we cannot comprehend from the Father who will fight to the death for us. In fact, he already did, and, because of his sacrifice on the cross for our sins, we do not have to live in the bondage that stress and spiritual warfare try to keep us in.

Through my most subconscious, dream-induced thoughts, God opened my eyes to show me that I had been living as an oppressed woman. Oppressed by anger. Oppressed by frustration, discouragement, hopelessness, and busyness. Oppressed by stress.

I had fought the battle of stress before on many occasions, but this go-round had been different. It had been more personal. It had been more emotionally damaging. This time it had involved pain, heartache, anger, and resentment, as opposed to just busyness. It had become a fierce battle—one that I was slowly losing—as I trudged through each day, unknowingly carrying the weight of the enemy's oppression.

I had given the devil a foothold in my life because I had not fully relied on the strongest weapon of all in this war against the unseen—God's Word. As a result, I had not guarded my heart against the enemy's tactics. Proverbs 4:23 instructs us, "Guard your heart above all else, for it determines the course of your life." I now understand the importance of this command more than ever before.

During the months prior to this God-inspired dream, I had been drowning in stress, from work, parenting, marital problems, worries, and problems beyond my ability to fix or control. Although I knew God instructs us to trust in our faith, not in our feelings (via Proverbs 3:5, "Trust in the LORD with all your heart; do not depend on your own understanding"), I was unaware of the toll my feelings had taken on my spirit. My feelings were running my life—or should I say *ruining* my life. Therefore, over a period of time, my negativity had erected an invisible wall that blocked my view of what God wanted to do in my life through my circumstances. A wall that blocked my view of seeing how much God loved me as my fears tried to convince me that he had abandoned me. Most importantly, it was blocking my ability to find peace amid my chaos. Stress took on a whole new meaning, and I wasn't making time for quiet time with God.

I had temporarily and inadvertently allowed the frustrations to become my focus, instead of the life-saving promises of the Bible. So although my physical body was not actually at war with the unseen enemy as it was in my dream, my spiritual body was. And the time came for God to pry away the life-robbing grip the devil had around my throat and remind me he does not leave his beloved ones to fight the battle alone. His Word, and all the truths tucked deep within every page and every verse, is the most powerful weapon we have to fight this battle of stress.

Through this dream experience, God blessed me with a glimpse of the unseen spiritual battle that takes place every day in our spirits as a result of the damaging effects of stressful situations in our lives that pull us away from God and the peace and strength available in him. He also blessed me with a reminder that when life gets stressful, the devil gets crafty. We need to realize who the real enemies are. Ephesians 6:12 says, "For we are not fighting against flesh-and-blood enemies, but against evil rulers and authorities of the unseen world, against mighty powers in this dark world, and against evil spirits in the heavenly places."

Spiritual warfare is often a subject people avoid for fear of being seen as "Jesus freaks" or religious fanatics if they talk about it. Or possibly because spiritual warfare is a hard subject to wrap our human minds around. But when our hearts are riddled with gaping holes from the battles we endure every day, I want you to know that the devil is most happy when you disregard his tactics as nothing more than tough luck. The enemy knows that if we don't acknowledge the invisible battle we are engaged in, and that we actually do have an enemy and unseen forces fighting against us, we will not reach for the weapons that will bring us victory. We will instead stand like a deer in an open field full of hunters—easy prey with nothing to protect us.

This battle is real, and it is stressful. It is a battle waged against us by the prince of this world through the adversities, circumstances, and heartaches we endure. It is a battle that keeps us busy and anxious so our spirits will become weary and frustrated. It is a battle we are hopeless to win unless we wrap ourselves in the promises and truths found on every single page of God's Word.

There is a battle going on for your mind and heart right now. You don't have to believe in spiritual warfare for the enemy to wage war on your life. In fact, he'd rather you not believe in it, because that makes his job much easier. But when it strikes, even when disguised as stress, you have the power within you and at your fingertips to fight it if you choose the right weapons.

Maybe you have felt unrest in your life lately, as I have so many times. Maybe you have felt oppressed and distant from God but haven't been able to pry yourself free from negative thoughts, painful memories, or emotions holding your heart captive and at arm's length from peace. Or perhaps you have been feeling confused, alone, and painfully distant from God, but you're unsure what steps to take to feel close to him again. Maybe your unwillingness to let go of anger or unforgiveness has built a wall you can no longer see over. Perhaps you feel as if you are imprisoned by the stress that hovers over your life, with no glimmer of hope for relief because you see no solution to or relief from your problems, with seemingly no light at the end of the tunnel. Or just maybe, you have accidentally, gradually, and unknowingly given the devil a foothold in your heart because you failed to guard it with the truths in God's Word. There has never been a better time than right now to surrender to God all that is weighing you down. If you only choose one weapon to fight off your stress, let God's Word be it.

Choose Spiritual Vitamins

About ten years ago, I experienced a serious tragedy—a hair tragedy, that is. I mean, it was serious to me at least.

I was only in my early forties, so in order to keep the gray hairs on my head at bay in the most cost-effective way, I had formed a monthly practice in my bathroom that involved some quality time with a box of Miss Clairol. One particular month, I got the great idea to try a slightly different color shade than usual in the hopes of brightening up my look, just a bit. Nothing could happen, right? Wrong.

After purchasing my new hair color choice and returning back home, I opened the box, mixed up the contents, and pulled on the flimsy, loose, plastic gloves before applying the color to my clean locks. I followed up that treatment with a new self-highlighting kit that I had bought at the same time, thinking a few highlights would give me a more trendy look. As if I had the skills of an experienced hairdresser. Mercy. Don't ask me what I was thinking.

After the allotted time period had passed, I showered, washed my hair, and wrapped a towel around my head as I went about the rest of my beauty routine. I stood in front of the mirror and removed the towel only to see an ugly, odd-colored mess sticking out from every direction. Pure panic set in, and, before you could say "hair color," I had put on a hat and was driving to the local drug store to get a new hair-color kit in my normal shade. But later that morning, after returning home, when I applied my usual shade on top of the mess I had created earlier, my hair came out looking even worse. Please don't ask me what I was thinking. My only excuse is that stress hormones were surging through my body, causing a near anxiety attack, which apparently severely impaired any form of rational thinking.

Before my wet hair even had time to dry, I had an emergency appointment made at a local salon. I knew this was a problem that could only be solved by a professional. Upon arriving at the salon, I tried to ignore the look of shock on my hairdresser's face as I tried to come up with excuses for my crazy, at-home hair-coloring antics. But she held her tongue, patted me on the shoulder, and sympathetically escorted me to her chair.

After assessing my situation, she determined that applying highlights and lowlights would repair the unnamed color on my head and get things back to normal again. Although I hesitantly agreed with her decision, for fear more bleach would cause even more damage, I pushed aside my concerns, trusting that she was the expert, and let her get to work.

When I left the salon, I was somewhat pleased with the results. I thought to myself, *Well, at least I no longer look like the perfect role model for a why-not-to-color-your-own-hair-at-home advertisement.* However, upon arriving home, my then eleven-year-old son took one look at my hair and exclaimed, "Mom, your hair looks like peanut butter and jelly." Gee . . . thanks, son. All the feels.

We laughed, or maybe I should say my family all laughed at my expense as I tried to be gracious. But what he meant was that the highlights, although they were soft brown and caramel colored, and not tannish nutmeg and purple colored, looked like the peanut butter and jelly that comes swirled together in a jar. Nonetheless, it was not a compliment I felt blessed to have received.

Several days passed and I was coping with my new hairdo just fine—until my peanut butter and jelly hair began falling out. Apparently, all that over-processing had caused so much damage, the hair all over my head began breaking off in large chunks from the scalp down. Within a couple of weeks, I went from having thick flowing hair down to my shoulders to an extremely short, chopped-up, multi-layered hairstyle. Although, calling it an actual "hairstyle" is a stretch.

I immediately established a hate–hate relationship with my hair (at least with what was left of it). I toyed with the idea of calling my hairdresser and giving her a piece of mind, since I was sure at least that would make me feel better, even though my hair tragedy wasn't entirely her fault.

For months I mourned over my hair loss. I despised looking at myself in the mirror because my hair was simply hideous! I managed it the best I could and hoped for quick hair growth and repair. But nothing worked. The damage was done, and now I was left to live with the consequences of my poor hair decisions. I had to succumb to the reality that all the wishing and moaning in the world was not going to get my old hair back, nor make it grow any faster.

After weeks of depression about my hair, waiting for it to grow back to no avail, I became desperate for a solution. I knew I had to do something other than whine and complain when my daughter exclaimed loudly, "If I hear you say one more time how much you hate your hair, I'm going to scream!" So I went online and ordered some expensive hair vitamins and an overpriced hair-repair conditioning system. I decided to put a serious focus on eating healthy and began exercising more, because I had heard both of those things helped foster the growth and strength of hair and nails.

As silly as it sounds, this upsetting hair situation—coupled with my overly busy life as a mom, wife, volunteer, speaker, and writer—had left me feeling discouraged, exhausted, stressed out, and fatigued. So, in addition to my hair vitamins, I purchased several general health vitamins, as well. I not only needed my hair back; I needed my energy back, too.

Little did I know these vitamins would have more benefits than originally thought. I gradually began feeling more energetic and realized my poor eating habits and lack of exercise had been affecting my stamina and zest for life. I noticed my fingernails seemed longer and thicker. But the best news of all was that, even though it took over a year to reach a noticeable turning point and multiple haircuts as all my many lengths tried to catch up to each other, my pitiful hair slowly began to grow back!

Although we've all heard we should take vitamins for better overall health and quality of living, I just didn't expect the obvious and immediate results that came from a concentrated effort to take better care of myself. As hard as it was to admit, I was almost thankful for the hair tragedy, because it opened my eyes to the importance of prioritizing our health and caring for our bodies.

I was prompted to consider what other areas of my life might be in need of a boost. What other areas could benefit from new zest energy? What other areas had I been ignoring that were in dire need of attention and, if given some, would have life-altering effects? The first thing that came to my mind was my walk with Jesus. My faith was a priority in my life; however, it had become routine and regular, instead of extraordinary and passionate. The thought of getting a spiritual boost was exciting, especially if my spiritual health could grow and improve as much as my physical health had. So I began pondering the idea of "spiritual vitamins" and making a list of ones I could take advantage of right away.

The next day, I started working through my list of ideas, with the first one being to call a few of my friends to lift me up in prayer. I knew if I was going to get intentional about boosting my relationship with Jesus, the devil would get intentional about preventing me from doing so. I was well aware I would need to be bathed in prayer if I planned to start leaning harder into my faith and seeking the level of peace and joy I once had before stress pushed them aside.

Next, I committed to reading my devotional each morning. I picked up a few new Christian book releases, which were each filled with encouragement from biblical principles and truths. Most importantly, I began reading God's Word again every day and making it a priority, pushing aside all excuses for why I might not have time.

I didn't just read the Bible out of obligation, but with a hunger to hear from God personally. I allowed his whispers to speak to my spirit, and each time I came across verses or passages I could apply to the circumstances I was facing, I made sure to never chalk it up to coincidence but "God incidence"—his voice speaking directly to my circumstances. I sought out his peace in my heart when my days were far from peaceful. And I attended a few powerful worship experiences, which rejuvenated my spirit and reenergized my soul.

After several months of getting into this new routine, I realized I not only felt physically better; I felt spiritually better too. The spiritual vitamins I had been ingesting every day had improved my spiritual health, just as I had hoped. They had become my most recent weapons against stress, discouragement, and frustration, and were helping me win the battle against the enemy, who wanted me to stay stressed, depressed, and anxious. I still had a million reasons to feel those emotions, but I had one reason why I didn't have to anymore.

First Peter 2:2 says, "Like newborn babies, you must crave pure spiritual milk so that you will grow into a full experience of salvation. Cry out for this nourishment." Peter knew that in order to stay close to Christ and be equipped to handle the problems and stress that life would bring, we would need to be fed spiritually on a daily basis.

If you are hungering for not only stress relief but also a renewed spirit and a healthier outlook on life, cry out for the nourishment that God provides. Determine what new routines (a.k.a. spiritual vitamins) you can prioritize in your own life, and invite God to start feeding your soul with much-needed nutrients. Just as tangible vitamins will improve your physical health, spiritual vitamins are guaranteed to improve your spiritual health. And, trust me, you will be amazed at the benefits you will reap.

Choose Prayer

I totally believe in the power of prayer. It is not just a religious duty; it is a spiritual privilege, knowing we are not merely talking *to* God but talking *with* God, and expecting to hear his reply.

In Psalm 86, we see a beautiful example of how we can pray, with both reverence and humanness. David's prayer begins by asking God to hear his pleas for protection, grace, and joy:

Bend down, O LORD, and hear my prayer; answer me,
for I need your help. Protect me, for I am devoted to you.
Save me, for I serve you and trust you. You are my God.
Be merciful to me, O Lord, for I am calling on you constantly. Give me happiness, O Lord, for I give myself to
you. O Lord, you are so good, so ready to forgive, so full of
unfailing love for all who ask for your help. Listen closely
to my prayer, O LORD; hear my urgent cry. (vv. 1–6)

Then, in the following verse, he acknowledges that he knows God
will answer: "I will call to you whenever I'm in trouble, and you
will answer me" (v. 7).

David admits his imperfections and his concerns and asks for
God's intervention. Although David often wavered in making good
decisions, he never wavered in believing God loved him despite his
sin. He was confident God heard his prayers, and confident God
would respond to them. David's hope was in God, and ours must
be too.

As believers, if we doubt whether or not God hears and will
respond to our prayers, then we need to question whether or not
we truly believe, because Scripture clearly states God hears our
prayers. Hebrews 4:16 says, "So let us come boldly to the throne of
our gracious God. There we will receive his mercy, and we will find
grace to help us when we need it most." First John 5:14 says, "This is
the confidence we have in approaching God: that if we ask anything
according to his will, he hears us" (NIV). Thus the problem is not
God's neglect of our needs or refusal to make his presence seen in
our life, but *our* neglect to pray and invite in him.

When my daughter Kaitlyn was in high school, we spent one
particular lazy Saturday hanging around the house. She had been
texting with a friend for hours on end over the course of the day.
Eventually, I leaned over and asked, "Are you seriously still talking
with her?" She nodded her head as she continued to look down at

her phone and type. I went on to say, "I just don't see how you can possibly have that much to talk about. Doesn't the conversation ever end?"

"Nope!" she proudly exclaimed. "We never really end the conversation or say good-bye. We just take breaks and then pick back up later where we left off." I rolled my eyes and suggested she force herself to take a break, or I might just help her take a really long break from her phone altogether.

We chuckled as she slid her phone into her pocket, but her answer piqued my interest and caused me to think about my conversations with God. How might my relationship with him grow if I simply never said *amen*? If I just kept the conversation going all day long, always picking back up where we left off or talking about new things?

In 1 Thessalonians 5:17, Paul gives us a very simple yet profound instruction: "Never stop praying." Here he is urging us to pray continually and never stop—not because God requires it but because our hearts long to feel close to him. Talking with God throughout the day invites him into even the smallest details of our lives. The Lord doesn't need us to pray continually to fill him in on what our problems, concerns, prayer requests, and praises are. Instead, we receive the blessing when we do so because we will feel his presence each and every day.

As I thought more about this, and thought how much time I would waste if I were texting my friends for hours and hours on end, I found myself coming up with excuses about why praying without ceasing wasn't really feasible. My mind started thinking too logically. *How can I possibly pray all the time, when I obviously have other thoughts going through my mind? How can I stay focused on prayer in the midst of the chaos of work, to-do lists, daily obligations, frustrations, parenting, and busyness?* How can I get anything else done if I'm sitting around praying all the time? I'm too busy for that! Don't I need to concentrate on other responsibilities? Won't that distract me from loving the ones I'm with? The more I thought about it, the more I realized something about myself. Deep down, my heart wanted to pray continually, and I knew there would be so many spiritual benefits of doing so. I wanted that close, intimate, friendship with God. So I dug a little deeper into the real meaning of Paul's instruction.

Praying continually doesn't mean we have to stay on our knees all day and pray without ever stopping, looking up, opening our eyes, or doing or thinking about anything else. It simply refers to having an attitude of prayer—to have a mindset that God is always near and present, like a trusted friend walking beside us or who is merely one text away at any given moment. A friend with whom we can jump back into the conversation whenever we're ready, with confidence that he will be eagerly listening.

The full context of 1 Thessalonians 5:16–18 says this: "Always be joyful. Never stop praying. Be thankful in all circumstances, for this is God's will for you who belong to Christ Jesus." You see, having a heart attitude of prayer simply means developing a focus on joy and gratitude grounded on a close relationship with our Savior. When we focus on the good and positive things as we walk through our busy days, instead of all the bad or stressful things all the time, which is a habit we can fall into, we can develop a mental attitude of thankfulness that gradually becomes second nature. When our hearts are full of thankfulness for God and his blessings, big and small, we will find ourselves longing to talk with him more and more and learning to recognize his holy whisper.

This longing to converse with him in any given moment, knowing he is listening, lays the groundwork for his peace to reside in our hearts, instead of stress, even during the most stressful of days. Never saying "amen" is one of the best, life-changing habits we can ever form and one of the greatest tools for inviting peace and rest into our lives.

But have no doubt, Satan will do everything in his power to distract us and keep us from having an attitude of prayer and thankfulness. The enemy knows the more time we spend talking with God, the more we will begin to depend on him and trust him with our whole hearts, lessening the gap for the enemy to sneak into our lives. But he can never keep God from hearing and answering our prayers, or keep us from hearing his voice in our spirits.

I can keep my daughter from having a never-ending texting conversation, but no one can keep us from having an ongoing conversation with the Most High. Nothing can stand in the way of us conversing with God unless we let it, and prayer is a conversation worth continuing, without ever saying "amen."

Maybe you have not chosen prayer as a weapon lately because you wonder if God really hears. If so, I want to assure you he does—not because I said so, but because God did. All throughout the Bible, we are reassured that God hears our prayers. One other example is found in Psalm 34:15: "The eyes of the LORD watch over those who do right; his ears are open to their cries for help."

Prayer is a powerful weapon nobody can ever take away from us, not even our worst enemy. It is a powerful and private conversation between us and the Sovereign Creator in which no one can intervene. If you have been struggling with prayer and believing God hears every word you think or speak, I have two suggestions. First, keep verse 11 from David's prayer in Psalm 86 in mind: "Teach me your ways, O LORD, that I may live according to your truth! Grant me purity of heart, so that I may honor you." David knew life was full of distractions, so he prayed for an undivided mind. He knew when life got hard or stressful, he might be tempted to focus on things other than God, so he prayed for the ability to live in God's ways and the strength to stay focused in his mind and heart. Second, pray without ceasing, and try with all your heart to never say amen. Prayer works. There is so much to say and so much to hear. Give it a try.

Choose Victory

They all started out in little ten-inch pots, but over a twenty-three-year period, each one had grown fifteen feet tall with a six-foot circumference. These four massive holly trees were now overtaking the front of my house, partially blocking my kitchen window, and slowly creeping closer and closer to my front door.

I finally bit the bullet and hired someone to cut them all down, cringing at how bare the front of the house was going to look, yet knowing I really had no other choice. I didn't realize the men who cut the trees down would leave the tree stumps in the ground, but I didn't think it was that big of a deal, so I just put it out of my mind.

You see, my noninformed self ignorantly assumed I could just cover them up with pine needles and forget about them. Which I did. Until, to my surprise, a few months later, little twigs and sprouts started poking up between the mounds of needles on all four stumps. After a little research, I discovered that unless you kill the root of a tree by treating its stump, rain and sunshine will bring life back to it and it will begin growing again.

As odd as it sounds, as I stood in my front yard sullenly staring at those sad, crooked stumps, only partially visible through the pine needles with little twigs sticking up, it occurred to me that my life was strikingly similar to those stumps. These trees had been chopped down to nothing. They had been stripped of every branch, twig, and leaf. If trees could be stressed, my poor holly trees had to be on the verge of a nervous breakdown.

I've had lots of stressful seasons during my lifetime, many of which I've shared here on these pages, but when my husband left our family, it was without a doubt the most stressful season I've ever endured. In fact, I remember feeling just like one of those stumps—chopped down as low as I could go and feeling like life was over. Damaged. Forgotten. Discarded. Covered up by darkness and despair, rather than pine needles, left wondering why God had allowed these painful circumstances into my life. Heartbroken, scared, and uncertain of the future, all because in one unforgettable day, my entire life was turned upside down and forever changed. I felt so hopeless and alone, and my stress, anxiety, and depression worsened with each passing day. I thought victory over my stress, much less victory in my life, would never be possible. I actually felt a little like Job in the Bible, because Scripture tells us that he felt the exact same way. He was a wealthy man who had everything, and life was good. Until it wasn't.

Job lost his ten children, his livestock, his servants, and his health. He literally lost everything, and although he was once like a massive tree full of life, in the course of one unforgettable day, he had been rendered nothing short of an old, dead stump. Yet, despite Satan's temptations to bring him down, Job fell to his knees instead. Rather than turning against God, as his friends and even his wife told him to do, he turned toward God, clinging to a hope that seems impossible, given his circumstances.

Job was only human, and Scripture documents how devastated and upset he was, even going so far as to curse the day he was born. His pain, thoughts, and emotions ran deep. But he still kept his faith; and eventually, he began to speak words of hope, believing that with God by his side, he could endure these tragic circumstances and grow and thrive again: "Even a tree has more hope! If it is cut down, it will sprout again and grow new branches" (Job 14:7). Job believed that despite the fact that he had lost everything, God was still God and he would survive.

Life's circumstances can feel so hard, unrelenting, and devastating. Whether it's divorce, health issues, financial struggles, the loss of a loved one, unemployment, or some other personal adversity, we often can't help but question why God is allowing us to suffer. We can't understand why he takes away the very things we treasure the most.

Even though your circumstances are likely entirely different than mine, perhaps you're feeling like an old dead stump right now.

Wondering if you can ever sprout twigs of life and happiness again, feeling hopeless and fearful about the future. Anxious and stressed. Overwhelmed with everything you have to face when you get out of bed each day. Maybe feeling as if victory over your life of stress is impossible for you, no matter how badly you want it.

Sweet friend, just like Job, you and I can decide to believe that despite our pain, what has happened to us, the problems we face, and the stressors we have to deal with, God is still a good God and he will never leave our side. If we want the stress-less life bad enough, longing to feel free, happy, and at peace despite our circumstances, we can choose to let our faith serve as hydration for our spirits and sunshine for our souls, so growth and new life can begin again. So victory can be had. Which is exactly what Job did.

Over time, God restored Job's health, gave him new children, provided him with twice the property he had lost, and granted him a long and happy life. While you're reading the story of Job in the Bible, taking in each verse that vividly describes his unending heartbreak, stress, anxiety, physical pain, loss, and so much more, you would never imagine in a million years that the day would come when our hero would have victory over his stress and live a life of peace and happiness. But he did. He held onto his faith, and over time, God restored Job's spirit and everything else in his life. Over time, God has also brought about great restoration in my life, and hanging onto hope carried me through, over the course of many years.

Victory over stress, anxiety, addiction to adrenaline, and even depression is possible for you, no matter how you feel right now or what you are going through. Romans 15:13 says, "May God, the source of hope, fill you with all joy and peace by means of your faith in him, so that your hope will continue to grow by the power of the Holy Spirit" (GNT). This hope Job had in God for peace, even amid the most stressful, traumatic, and trying season of his life—the same hope I had in my darkest, most stressful days during the hardest years I've ever endured, the hope that every character in the Bible and every Christian who has ever lived has ever had—is the same hope that is available to you. A pure unconditional hope, which leads to peace defined as the absolute victory over stress.

If this is true (which it is!), why do most of us search everywhere else for stress relief, except God? Why do we reach for every weapon against stress available, except the Bible and closeness with God? Why do we spend time searching for something, or someone, that can save us from our stress, falsely believing some temporary pleasure or sense of relief is going to bring lasting peace? Why do we live out every day as if there is no hope to overcome our chaos and no possibility for living a stress-less life when Scripture repeatedly reassures us that God has the power and the peace to make that happen? The answer is simple—in the same way we may feel that prayer doesn't work, we may not believe God is powerful enough to handle our problems, so we resolve to live in a sea of despair and stress and just try to keep from drowning. Or we simply lose sight of the fact that he is sovereign and in control, because we are so busy trying to control and manage everything ourselves.

God has the power to calm the storms in your life. He has the sovereignty to crush the inner demons you are battling against. He always has victory over the enemy, and he has already won the battle. He has been, is, and always will be triumphant.

God can effortlessly still the brutal waves in the raging sea of our lives, but we have to put our lives in his hands before he can do so. It's time to take a deep breath and rest in knowing that he will have victory, in his perfect timing and in his perfect ways, if you give him a chance to go to battle for you.

If you are searching for a weapon to fight your stress, don't look to the ways of the world. Don't let society or the enemy of our souls convince you that drugs, alcohol, physical pleasures, or random coping mechanisms are the only choices you have to survive a life of stress. Don't fall for the lies that you can't escape a life of stress and that living in a chronic state of anxiety, feeling overwhelmed, overloaded, frazzled, and fatigued is normal. Instead, choose to make God a priority, choose to spend time with his Word every day, choose to pray without ceasing, and choose to invest in a routine of spiritual vitamins. As you fight the battle with these tools, you will also be simultaneously choosing your victory.

Reflection Questions

1. Ponder the thought of spiritual warfare with regard to any difficult situations you have been struggling with lately. Have you considered that these adversities could be spiritual warfare, rather than "tough luck"? Ask God to provide you with spiritual clarity. Take some time to research God's Word along with Bible commentaries to obtain a deeper understanding of the enemy's ways so that you can be more aware and better spiritually prepared for the enemy's attacks in the future. Jot down any notes or thoughts here.

2. Make a list of "spiritual vitamins" that you can begin taking to help give your spiritual walk with God a boost. Consider things like more fellowship with other believers, attending church more regularly, going to revivals and new Bible studies, and making time for daily devoted quiet time, focused prayers, daily online devotionals, etc. Put them in order of priority to you, and commit to start taking at least one new vitamin this week.

3. What does spiritual strength mean to you? After you define spiritual strength from your perspective, list a few ways that you have exhibited spiritual strength in difficult situations in the past. Write a brief prayer, praising God for helping you get through those situations in his strength.

4. If God were to take a snapshot of you right now, what would his picture show? List a few adjectives that might describe your photo, even if they are not positive descriptions. (Be sure to use this as a self-assessment, a tool that will push you toward a goal of spiritual growth, not as a list of reasons to practice self-condemnation.)

5. Now consider what you would like for God's picture of you to look like. Write down the strengths or positive attributes that you want God to help you develop.

6. If the picture of your reality is not a picture of God's strength working within you, how can you begin making some positive changes to build your dependence and trust in God? What situations or issues do you need to turn over to God, humbly admitting that you don't have the strength to persevere without him?

7. What are the main obstacles standing in the way of you surrendering your stressors to God and inviting his peace into your
heart? Write down the first things that come to mind. Take time to
turn them over to God, asking him to bring victory over those lies
and convert your heart from one with a spirit of doubt and stress
to a spirit of peace and victory.

Stress-Busting Scriptures

*The LORD is my light and my salvation—whom shall I fear? The
LORD is the stronghold of my life—of whom shall I be afraid?*

Psalm 27:1 NIV

❧

God is our refuge and strength, an ever-present help in trouble.

Psalm 46:1 NIV

❧

*Do not be afraid, for I have ransomed you. I have called you
by name; you are mine. When you go through deep waters,
I will be with you. When you go through rivers of difficulty,
you will not drown. When you walk through the fire of oppression,
you will not be burned up; the flames will not consume you.
For I am the LORD, your God, the Holy One of Israel, your Savior.*

Isaiah 43:1b–3a

❧

*The God of peace will soon crush Satan under your feet.
May the grace of our Lord Jesus be with you.*

Romans 16:20

❧

Be on guard. Stand firm in the faith. Be courageous. Be strong.

1 Corinthians 16:13

❧

*Always be joyful. Never stop praying.
Be thankful in all circumstances, for this is God's will
for you who belong to Christ Jesus.*

1 Thessalonians 5:16–18

❧

CHAPTER NINE

Hitting the Reset Button

Most of us desperately want to feel capable of handling the trials and problems of life on our own. We want to feel equipped to deal with what life throws at us, and we take pride in our accomplishments when we do so. But it is often that exact determination and pride that causes unnecessary stress. In fact, some of us would rather risk falling flat on our faces than admit we need help.

When we get caught up in this battle of wills, God sometimes allows us to get to our breaking point before he steps in, but he does it for our own benefit, not out of spite or lack of love. Until we recognize we are utterly helpless on our own, we won't be able to understand we really have no control over life. Our pain and suffering will serve as a catapult to drive us toward God, and when we begin to see him, our hope will be renewed.

One great example of finding hope when we least expect it is found in 1 Kings 17, where we learn of a widow who was broken and had lost all hope. In this chapter, the prophet Elijah was told by God to take a trip to Zarephath in the region of Sidon, and God promised that he would provide for his needs while he was gone. In keeping with his Word as he always does, God divinely arranged for a widow to supply Elijah's food and housing needs when he reached Zarephath.

Upon arriving at Zarephath, although he did not know for sure that this was part of God's plan and provision for him, Elijah saw the widow picking up sticks and asked her for some food. In 1 Kings 17:12, the widow replied to Elijah by saying, "As surely as the LORD your God lives . . . I don't have any bread—only a handful of flour in a jar and a little oil in a jug. I am gathering a few sticks to take home and make a meal for myself and my son, that we may eat it—and die" (NIV).

Is it just me or does that sound just a bit overly dramatic—like something a teenager would say if she was told she couldn't go out with her friends on Friday night? "Mom, if I don't get to go, I might die!" The widow's reply sounds borderline drama queen, yet also sounds a tad sarcastic, but I feel sure that, in either case, it was not the response Elijah expected. In thinking about this, I began to wonder what tone she actually used when making this statement to Elijah.

Maybe she said it with great bitterness and anger in her heart, shaking her fist at God, wondering why he had let her husband die—leaving both she and her son without food. Maybe she said it with sarcasm, knowing that she probably would not really die after her next meal, but life was such a struggle, that she would not care either way. Maybe she was just being honest, knowing their malnutrition was growing worse and honestly believing any meal could potentially be their last. Or maybe she said it in great despair, with her head hung low, tears falling from her eyes, full of hopelessness and sadness, not wanting to die but seeing no way out. And since no solution seemed within her reach, she had already surrendered to that imminent fate.

We have no idea how this poor woman was really feeling, but what we *do* know is God had not forgotten her. He knew she was in the deepest stress of her life. And although she probably thought

God did not care about her situation, and she felt ignored, forgotten, stressed, and overcome with fear and anxiety, he had already made plans for her miracle to occur in his perfect timing.

First Kings 17:13–16 reads:

> Elijah said to her, "Don't be afraid. Go home and do as you have said. But first make a small cake of bread for me from what you have and bring it to me, and then make something for yourself and your son. For this is what the Lord, the God of Israel, says: 'The jar of flour will not be used up and the jug of oil will not run dry until the day the Lord gives rain on the land.'"
>
> She went away and did as Elijah had told her. So there was food every day for Elijah and for the woman and her family. For the jar of flour was not used up and the jug of oil did not run dry, in keeping with the word of the Lord spoken by Elijah. (NIV)

Even though this woman's circumstances seemed grim, causing her to lose all hope of getting out of the pit she had found herself in, which was of no fault of her own, God had a plan. He had ordained Elijah to meet this widow at an appointed day and time. And as she carried out her routine tasks, just like any other day, God put his plan, her miracle, into place.

We are not told in this Scripture this widow had been seeking God's intervention. In fact, we could safely assume she did not even know the Lord, since, when she spoke to Elijah, she made the comment in verse 12, "As surely as the Lord *your* God lives." Notice she didn't say "my God," but instead she referred to God as the Lord of Elijah. Conversely, she probably worshiped the idol Baal. But the Lord still saw her suffering and cared about her nonetheless. Despite what some people tend to believe, God truly does love and shows himself to all people because he wants every person to put their faith in him (Matt. 5:45).

God also reiterates his love for all people in Romans 2:4, where it says, "Don't you see how wonderfully kind, tolerant, and patient God is with you? Does this mean nothing to you? Can't you see that his kindness is intended to turn you from your sin?" God is merciful and loving to all people, whether they believe in him or not, yet his desire is that all will come to know him through this mercy. And sometimes he uses stressful situations to help them do that.

God was kind to the widow and provided for her physical, emotional, and spiritual needs. He eliminated the physical sources of stress in her life (finances and food) and provided a spiritual source of strength by allowing her to witness miracles, through Elijah, but that only God could do. He gave her victory over the stress in her life and, most importantly, the stress in her heart.

Maybe you can relate to the feelings the widow expressed to Elijah. When faced with overwhelming despair and stress, it is normal to feel hopeless and defeated, wondering what tomorrow holds—or if there will even be a tomorrow. But I urge you to focus on the truth despite what you are going through. And the truth is that God has a miracle planned for you too, if you are willing to expect it, look for it, and wait for it to play out in God's perfect timing. Don't fall into the trap of thinking your problems are too big for God, because no matter how big they seem, God is bigger. He is capable of giving you victory over your stress and filling your deepest desires for peace and rest in your heart and life. The first step toward claiming that victory is believing it can happen for you because of who God is.

If you are in a pit of stress or despair, don't succumb to defeat. Don't accept that difficult place as your fate. Even though God has allowed you to be there right now, he never intended for you to live there. The only way to see past the problem is to believe that he has not forgotten or abandoned you and that, at the exact time that he has ordained, he will reach down and pick you up. Just as a mother would never forget her own child, God never forgets his children.

And even if you have not been looking for him or seeing him, he has seen you. He knows what you are going through and the stress you are under. He knows how desperately you long to feel at peace in your heart, soul, and mind. And he is ready to answer your prayers whenever you're ready to invite him to get to work in your life and stop trying to do it all via your own strength and power.

Tips to Begin the Reset of Your Life

We all get stuck in ruts from time to time and find ourselves in situations we want out of. In fact, we have all probably felt like the widow with the sticks, like David facing Goliath, or like Hannah facing infertility and verbal persecution, even though our circumstances are entirely different. The stress of today's society couldn't have even been imagined in biblical times, especially considering the astronomical increase in stress statistics over the past couple of years due to the global pandemic and political unrest. I shared a lot of statistics earlier in this book, but one of the most alarming ones I came across that the majority of us share is the fear of uncertainty of the future. In 2020, the APA's Stress in America study obtained the following results:

> Nearly 2 in 3 adults (65 percent) say the current amount of uncertainty in our nation causes them stress. Further, 3 in 5 (60 percent) say the number of issues America faces currently is overwhelming to them. This finding speaks to the hardships many Americans may be confronting at this moment. Issues they are stressed about are not going away, they are piling up.
>
> Along with the personal and national issues that are causing them significant stress, Americans now also are more commonly worried about the long-term well-being of the country. More than 3 in 4 adults (77 percent) say the future of our nation is a significant source of

stress, up significantly from 2019 when 66 percent of adults said the same. And more than 7 in 10 Americans (71 percent) say this is the lowest point in our nation's history that they can remember. In 2019, only 56 percent of Americans shared this sentiment.[15]

We all have a lot of problems and stressors in our lives. Some we feel we can manage them or that they will resolve themselves in time; others are completely and utterly out of our control. But if there is one stressor we all share, as evidenced by these studies, it is the uncertain state of our nation, what the future will look like for our families, and the sacredness of our freedoms. Stressors that we have zero power to manage, control, or fix, and knowing we have no power to change them, can cause even more anxiety. In fact, even just watching the news can cause anxiety levels to spike in my heart and probably yours too, because despite how upset you can become because of what you hear, there is nothing at all you can do about it. But stress.

Or we can choose not to. The choice is always ours.

In this world of chaos, stress, worries, and busyness that we live in, it's so easy to get off track and be pulled onto a path we would have never deliberately chosen. No one wants to live a stressed-out life, and I would venture to say that in most cases, people fall into lives of stress by accident, oftentimes due to circumstances that were not even their fault or that they never saw coming. Or maybe we got so caught up running through life like a freight train, thinking we are immune to the disease of stress, that we allowed the twists and turns of life to blind us to the potential dangers ahead. Or perhaps some of us saw all the warning signs that danger was ahead and knew stress was affecting our mental, emotional, spiritual, and physical health, but we failed to steer ourselves away from it because we didn't see any way to stop the train.

In any case, when we find ourselves at the end of our rope, it's safe to say we probably all secretly wish we had a reset button for our lives, allowing us the opportunity to go back in time and make better decisions about the paths we have taken. We just want to start all over with a clean slate and a fresh opportunity to approach each day differently and intentionally avoid stress, which robs us of peace and steals our happiness. We want to be able to live the abundant life God promises.

Although there is no official reset button, there are things we can do to "reboot" our lives and jump-start the process of getting back on track to a life that is filled with peace and joy. The first of those I've already mentioned, which involves choosing the right weapons to carry with us throughout each day. But there are also tangible actions we can put into place if we are truly ready to change how we live and make the best of the life we still have.

Here are five action items that, if you are willing to implement them into your everyday life, will serve as crucial stepping stones toward achieving your goal of living a stress-less life.

Remember the Treasure

Your word is a lamp to guide my feet and a light for my path.

Psalm 119:105

All too often our Bibles are nothing more than a pretty book that sits on the coffee table collecting dust. We may carry it back and forth to church, but we don't really consider it a resource tool for living. But what if we realigned our lives according to God's Word? What if we began to consider the Bible our only lifeline? What if we gave it the importance it actually deserved? Would our lives be different?

When pondering these questions for myself, I remembered a meaningful encounter I experienced with my son right after he turned six years old.

Every year my church held a special annual recognition cere-mony, giving out Bibles to rising first graders. When this designated Sunday finally arrived, little Michael was beaming with excitement. He could not wait to receive his very own special Bible.

The children's minister began calling out the names of children one by one, and each child excitedly skipped down to the front of the church to accept his or her new Bible. My son sat there quietly but squirming in the pew with anticipation, anxiously awaiting the sound of his name. When it was called, he jumped up, looked straight at me, and gave me a huge ear-to-ear grin. You would have thought he had won tickets to Disney World based on the joy on his little face!

He received his crisp new Bible and then skipped back to the pew where we were sitting. For the next thirty minutes, as the pastor shared his message with the congregation, Michael admired his Bible. He held it close to him. He hugged it lovingly. He caressed it. He flipped through all the pages looking for pictures of the Bible stories he recognized. He smelled the fresh, crisp pages. He even kissed it over and over with silly little head bobbing motions. He was so proud of and in love with his new Bible!

At home later that afternoon, he picked up his Bible and looked up at me with eyes wide open, saying with great emphasis, "Mom, did you know that I have *God's. Holy. Word.* right in my hands?"

My motherly heart melted, and tears came to my eyes. Yet as I witnessed a passion for Jesus and the Word of God in the heart of my child, I felt a twinge of guilt spread over my own spirit—I considered how long it had been since I treasured God's Word that passionately. My son reminded me just how precious God's Word should be to us. Although he was too young at that time to fully understand all the lessons the Bible teaches us, he knew in his innocent little heart that it was invaluable. If only life could stay as simple as it was when we were six years old.

With growth comes problems, and stress. And with all those stumbling blocks and realities of adulthood we have to manage, it's all too easy to fall out of love with God's Word and forget what a gift it is. Forget it is the one thing that will keep our stress at bay and our hearts in the right place, allowing our lives to get off track and out of alignment. We slowly lose sight of the peace it holds tucked within the pages, and then eventually, we can lose his peace completely.

Consider whether your life is aligned with the Word of God, and ask God to show you where changes need to be made. When was the last time you hugged your Bible close to your heart, simply because your heart melted at knowing what a treasure it was? When was the last time you paused long enough to breathe, take a hard look at your life, and assess what or who was guiding your actions and decisions on a daily basis—and, in turn, affecting your peace and happiness?

Time spent with God is always time well spent—so set a goal to get reconnected with his Word. If you think you simply don't have time in your schedule, therein lies proof that it is the exact thing you need to do. The Bible is a treasure that holds the secret to a peace-filled, less-stressed life.

Recognize Your Need
May your mercy come quickly to meet us,
for we are in desperate need.
Psalm 79:8b NIV

Why is it that we so often have to be at the end of our rope before we feel desperate enough to call for help? Just as stress is a disease that takes its toll on our overall existence, self-sufficiency syndrome is a disease of the heart, as well. This syndrome is characterized by our desire to handle everything on our own, afraid to show any sign of weakness or neediness to anyone, including God. God never meant for us to be self-sufficient. Dependable, yes. Responsible, yes. Confident, yes. Self-sufficient, no.

John 15:5 says, "Yes, I am the vine; you are the branches. Those who remain in me, and I in them, will produce much fruit. For apart from me you can do nothing." Why do we try to do things on our own when God's Word explicitly states we cannot do anything apart from him? Ask God to be your strength and deliverer; commit to depending on him first, even when you think you can "do it all by yourself." Because no matter how hard you try, how much you've accomplished, how many degrees you have, how strong or confident you are . . . the day will come when you realize he was right all along. The sooner we realize our need for him, the sooner we can begin to live happier, more peaceful lives, even if our circumstances remain chaotic.

Adjust Your Focus

Have you never heard? Have you never understood?
The Lord is the everlasting God, the Creator of all the earth.
He never grows weak or weary. No one can measure
the depths of his understanding.

Isaiah 40:28

When change becomes necessary, that change often needs to begin with a look at where we are placing our focus. It's better to do it sooner than wait until the breaking point, but when the time does come when we reach our wit's end and our stress is taking a negative toll on our bodies, lives, relationships, jobs, and more, we need to take a hard look at where we are placing our focus. Are we focusing on our circumstances and all things out of our control to manage, or are we focusing on God and trusting in his abilities to handle all things, even those that seem impossible?

I once heard my pastor say, "Trouble and adversity are like bananas—they come in bunches." This statement rings so true—it always seems that when one stressful situation reaches the maximum level, another stressful situation falls in right behind it. I have found this to be true in my life. In my profession, for example, where I juggle multiple responsibilities of working full-time, being an author with several contracts, working as a writing mentor, and other duties, I often find myself feeling overwhelmed and wishing I had three of me to get all the work done. I tell myself things will be better in a few months when I get certain projects behind me, but it never fails that as soon as one project deadline is met, another deadline looms. The same can happen in our personal lives: We get through one difficult season, thinking we've finally made it to easier times, but then an unexpected issue falls in our lap out of nowhere and we find ourselves right back in the pit of anxiety yet again. There will always be something to stress about, and we will never be without stressful circumstances in our lives, which is exactly why it's so important to ground ourselves and our faith so we can maintain a peace that surpasses even during the most difficult seasons of life.

When we constantly focus on the carousel of stressful circumstances always spinning in our lives instead of trusting that God is in control and focusing on how he is at work, forgetting that he is there, we can and will eventually become overwhelmed. Worry, fear, and anxiety will continue to be peace stealers.

It's not always easy—in fact, it's not ever easy—but try to remind yourself each morning when you wake up to focus on God and the fact that he promises you peace, no matter what that day may hold.

Be Faithful in Your Prayer Life

Let us then approach the throne of grace with confidence,
so that we may receive mercy and find grace
to help us in our time of need.

Hebrews 4:16 NIV

What a privilege and a blessing to be given permission by God to approach his throne of grace, but what a shame that we often take this awesome opportunity for granted. God created us with an innate desire to be connected to him. When we fail to do so, an emptiness forms in our hearts, and our enemy is more than glad to fill it with things other than God.

God answers prayers, in his ways and in his timing. But if we fail to pray, he has nothing to act upon.

Philippians 4:6–7 reads, "Don't worry about anything; instead, pray about everything. Tell God what you need, and thank him for all he has done. Then you will experience God's peace, which exceeds anything we can understand. His peace will guard your hearts and minds as you live in Christ Jesus."

Remember what we talked about earlier regarding never saying "amen"? Give it a shot this week. Start up a conversation and pour out your heart to God. When you're out of words, just say, "See ya later," and ask God to walk beside you for the rest of the day. The next time a thought or concern comes to mind, strike up the conversation again—in the same way you would pick up your phone and text a friend when you remembered something you wanted to tell them.

Prayer doesn't have to be a formal presentation with a specific beginning, middle, and end. It simply needs to come from your heart straight to God's. Just remembering he is there, ready to listen at any given moment, never hanging up or saying good-bye, can provide a sense of peace you may have never experienced before.

Believe God Is Who He Says

When Jesus came to the region of Caesarea Philippi, he asked his disciples, "Who do people say that the Son of Man is?" "Well," they replied, "some say John the Baptist, some say Elijah, and others say Jeremiah or one of the other prophets." Then he asked them, "But who do you say I am?" Simon Peter answered, "You are the Messiah, the Son of the living God."

Matthew 16:13–16

When life gets hard, we tend to start doubting that God is God. We secretly entertain the lie that, just maybe, he isn't really in control. If he were, why are so many hard things happening? Why isn't he intervening? Why can't we see him fixing our problems, lessening our worries, answering our prayers? We begin to wonder whether he is truly big enough to fix our problems after all. Or, at a minimum, we wonder if he is taking time to see us and care about what we're going through. But God is who he says he is, all the time.

In Revelation 1:8, God reminds us of who he is: "'I am the Alpha and the Omega—the beginning and the end,' says the Lord God. 'I am the one who is, who always was, and who is still to come—the Almighty One.'" God is always God, despite our circumstances.

What we view as God's absence or lack of quickness to change our circumstances or fix our problems is really God waiting for the proper time to act on our behalf, waiting for us to acknowledge our need for rescue, or divinely orchestrating a better plan than we asked for because his ways are so much better than ours.

Second Peter 3:9 says, "The Lord isn't really being slow about his promise, as some people think. No, he is being patient for your sake. He does not want anyone to be destroyed, but wants everyone to repent." If he "fixed" our problems overnight, would our love of him or our dependence on him grow? If he answered every wish or prayer exactly as we asked, in our preferred time frame, would we really be grateful for his sovereign goodness? Might we even start to give ourselves credit for the things that are going well in our lives, instead of him? True faith depends on believing God is God, even when we feel he isn't paying attention to our pleas or working in our lives.

Think back to a time when you prayed a prayer that God answered, or when you saw in hindsight how God had been weaving together a plan over time, which you would have never fathomed but which turned out to be a blessing in your life. Remember those times when your faith starts waning or your stress begins planting seeds of doubt of his faithfulness and goodness. Those memories can reignite your faith and give you the strength to pick yourself up and keep going, just one more day, knowing he has never and will never leave your side.

Unbelief and doubt put our circumstances between us and God; faith puts God between us and our circumstances. If you are serious about "resetting" your life, put God first and ask him to free you from any doubts about his faithfulness. Never doubt he is who he says he is. In addition to making your faith a priority, it's important to make yourself a priority as well. The following are a few tips on how to do start doing just that—simple suggestions, but things we tend to let slip to the back-burner if we don't purposefully prioritize ourselves and our health.

Know when you're entering the stress zone. Just like when I was watching the chaos of the raid on the capitol building, well aware that my blood pressure was rising and my anxiety increasing, along with all those seasons of life when I was acutely aware my health issues were specifically related to my stress levels, it is crucial that you live aware of when you are overly stressed. Don't ignore the cues and red flags your body is throwing up. Develop an awareness of how you feel in stressful situations—emotionally, physically, and mentally. Have a plan in place for what to do when you realize your stress or anxiety is reaching dangerous levels, so when it does happen, you'll be prepared to deal with it and cope in a healthy way.

Have an accountability partner. Having someone to help us stay accountable to any goal we set for ourselves is vital to success. Create a stress support system for yourself, composed of one or more friends you can call on when you're on the verge of letting stress take over again. You could also consider forming a habit of getting together weekly to talk about life and stressors, because talking through our problems helps keep our emotions and anxiety from staying locked inside until we reach a breaking point. If you ever need it, don't be too proud to seek professional help. God can work miracles through the medical professionals he put here on earth for our benefit.

Always plan for "me" time. Yes, time for little ol' you. You deserve it. If you're like me, you could rattle off twenty reasons in twenty seconds of why you don't have time to make time for yourself, but the benefits of forcing yourself to take time away and reboot far outweigh the costs. Even if you feel a little stressed at first, thinking about the responsibilities you'll be putting off for a bit, you'll return from your "me" time refreshed, less stressed, and even be more productive than you would have been otherwise. Just as our bodies need rest after a long day, our brains need rest in order to concentrate and think clearly, so downtime and time alone allow your brain to recharge.

Laugh until your sides hurt. There is nothing I love more than a funny comedy movie that makes me laugh until I cry, or a fun weekend with my girlfriends, filled with laughter and good times. Laughter actually reduces the level of stress hormones that cause so much damage to our bodies when they remain in our system too long (cortisol and epinephrine) and increases our levels of feel-good hormones (like endorphins and neurotransmitters), all of which lead to a stronger immune system and better health! This is backed up by Scripture in Proverbs 17:22: "If you are cheerful, you feel good; if you are sad, you hurt all over" (CEV). Laughter is good for the soul!

Dare not to compare. Oh, how much time and energy we waste trying to keep up with the Joneses, be just like "her," put our kids on as many sports teams as everyone else, work more overtime, keep a cleaner house, have the perfect social media photos—striving to be better and do more. Always looking around to see if we are doing enough, being enough. Comparing ourselves to everyone around us and convincing ourselves we have to keep up an unhealthy pace of life and dangerous levels of stress because everyone else does and they seem to be handling it just fine. Yet, behind closed doors, the reality is they are probably not. Theodore Roosevelt once said, "Comparison is the thief of joy." Nothing is more dangerous than feeling "less than" because we look at others and think they are somehow "more than." That misconception tempts us to live a life of stress to try to be who we *think* we should be, rather than who we *want* to be and who God has called us to be. Enjoy your life, the one God has given you, and never let the comparison trap suck you into a stress zone where you don't belong and don't need to be in order to be happy. Living with peace is a choice. It is a gift we must ask for and strive to maintain daily, but it is a choice nonetheless.

Reflection Questions

1. Is your Bible collecting dust or collecting turned-down pages? Whatever the "collection" is, is a reflection of how you are viewing the treasure God has given you. What steps can you take to reconnect with the Word of God and make it more of a priority in your life?

2. What is your greatest need right now, either physically or emotionally? Do you trust God can meet that need? Write a brief prayer confessing your dependency on God and committing to trust his ways and his timing.

3. In your desperation to manage your life and handle stress the best way you know how, have you become so focused on your problems you've lost focus on who is in control? Have you become too self-sufficient? Do you need to surrender your life and your issues to God, giving him an opportunity to work in your life? Write down your thoughts here.

4. How would you describe your prayer life lately? How does thinking about talking to God without saying good-bye, or amen, make praying and going to him seem a little easier or more natural? Commit to starting a new habit of conversing in prayer today, and ask God to help you be more aware of his presence as you walk more closely with him throughout each day.

5. Which of the self-care tips listed in this chapter do you think you need to implement in your life today? Think of a few ways you can begin doing these immediately, making yourself and your mental, emotional, and physical health a priority. We are never any good to others if we don't first take care of ourselves.

6. If you have still not accepted Jesus Christ into your heart as your personal Savior, will you pause and do that right now? He has been waiting for you to discover that he is the answer you have been so desperately seeking. Your stress, anxiety, chaos, and busyness are merely symptoms of the absence of his hand in your life. He is standing with open arms, waiting to welcome you into his Kingdom. If your heart has been moved and you feel a desire and a need to truly invite Jesus into your life, will you say the prayer below? There is no right or wrong way to pray this prayer of salvation and commitment to Jesus. View this prayer as an opportunity to admit your need for God and invite him into your life without worrying over eloquent words or church-sounding statements. Jesus is not concerned with how we talk to him—just that we do.

Heavenly Father, have mercy on me, a sinner. I believe you are the one true God. I believe the Holy Bible is infallible and every word is true. I believe Jesus Christ is the Son of the living God and that he died on the cross so I may have forgiveness for my sins and eternal life in heaven. I know without you in my heart, Lord, my life is meaningless and without purpose. Forgive me for my unbelief in the past, or at least for forgetting you are who say you are and you are worthy of being trusted with my circumstances, so I don't have to suffocate under the weight of stress every day.

I believe in my heart that Jesus was raised from the dead and sits at your right hand. Please forgive me for every sin I have ever committed in thought or deed. Please come into my heart as my personal Lord and Savior today. I need you to be my Father, and I want you to be my best friend, fostering an intimate relationship with me.

I give you my life and ask you to take full control from this moment on. I am excited about the new life I will have in you. I pray all this in the name of Jesus Christ. Amen.

If you said this prayer today, welcome to the family of God. You have experienced a breakthrough, and your brokenness has made you whole.

Stress-Busting Scriptures

For God so loved the world that he gave his one and only Son, that whoever believes in him shall not perish but have eternal life.

John 3:16 NIV

Jesus answered, "I am the way and the truth and the life. No one comes to the Father except through me."

John 14:6 NIV

For I will pour out water to quench your thirst and to irrigate your parched fields. And I will pour out my Spirit on your descendants, and my blessing on your children.

Isaiah 44:3

Jesus replied, "I am the bread of life. Whoever comes to me will never be hungry again. Whoever believes in me will never be thirsty."

John 6:35

And the Holy Spirit helps us in our weakness. For example, we don't know what God wants us to pray for. But the Holy Spirit prays for us with groanings that cannot be expressed in words.

Romans 8:26

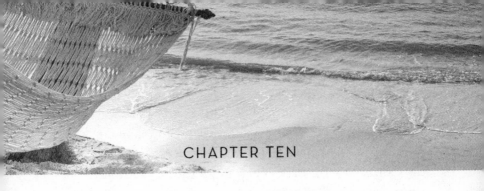

CHAPTER TEN

Embracing Your Stress-Less Life

Let's pretend for a moment my name is Martha and I have a very large group of people coming over to my house for a dinner party, including a very special guest. I will make no plans for several days before the guests are supposed to arrive because I know my house will need a serious floor to roof cleaning—I'm going to be busy.

Tubs and toilets have rings around them that must be scrubbed and bleached. Carpets need to be vacuumed. But before any of this can be done, my children have a lot of work to do cleaning their rooms and picking up their myriad of personal items that have been carelessly strewn about the house.

All the hardwood floors need a good hands-and-knees spot cleaning in preparation for mopping and waxing to take place. I decided long ago my house is the dust magnet of the universe, so a lot of dusting will most certainly need to be done.

The window blinds have not been washed in so long they are starting to look cream instead of white, and the stairs will need a good sweeping. I recently noticed when the sun shines in, it illuminates the fingerprints on the windows, so each of the windows needs to be cleaned. The kids have dripped drinks and other liquid items down the kitchen cabinets, so all the cabinets will need to be wiped down, and a good coat of wood polish would even make them shine again.

The oven needs to be cleaned, since last week's lasagna drippings nearly caused a house fire. I noticed a few Christmas tree needles were still behind the couch, even though Christmas was months ago, so certainly all the furniture will need to be moved so I can clean behind and under everything.

I definitely need to make sure all the dirty clothes are washed and put away, so my laundry room will look as if I never use it. Since the curtains in the house haven't been washed in ten years, I probably should take them all down, wash, and iron them.

The front porch needs to be swept. And the garage, too. But first I'll need to organize all the beach chairs, power tools, basketballs, bicycles, and muddy shoes that call the garage their home, just in case any of my guests want to enter my house through the garage door. If the weather is nice, my guests might want to venture outside for some fresh air, so I better sweep the deck, too. Oh yeah, and wipe down all the deck furniture and then wash all the chair cushions.

Now for the exterior. I recently noticed that a few of our house shingles were loose, so I'll need to call someone to repair those. Ten bales of pine straw must be ordered for the front lawn, and new pansies planted around the mailbox would make a great impression when people approach the house, as long as I pull out all the weeds that grew up over the winter. And the driveway could use a good pressure wash. Oh, and I need to make a mental note to call the neighborhood boy who mows the lawn.

After spending hours doing Internet searching, I will hopefully find several delectable gourmet recipes I would probably never make for my own family. I'll type up my list and head to the grocery store. I'll need to add new kitchen towels to that list, since all the ones I have look as if they have spent some time in a blender. Then, when I get home, I will devote at least three hours to preparing appetizers and making sure they are strategically organized into glorious edible designs on the wedding china, which has never been used. Then it's on to tackling the feat of cooking the main entrees.

On the day of the dinner party, I will surely be exhausted, to say the least. My family will be avoiding me by now, for fear I might ask them to do some form of housework. On top of all this, they'll be terrified they might accidentally spill something on my shiny, freshly waxed floors, provoking an outburst or mental meltdown.

When my guests finally arrive, including my very special guest, I will be thrilled! However, I will probably be too tired to get up and meet them at the door. I am sure they will marvel at how clean my house is and how wonderful my food looks and shower me with compliments and appreciation. And, if anyone who lives in my humble abode tries to sit around lazily and not help out while our guests are here, they'd better be ready for a tongue-lashing.

Then, after all that, hopefully I will still have enough energy left to sit with Jesus, my special guest. I'd love to talk quietly with him and soak in his peace and wisdom. But I imagine by that time, I'll just be way too tired. Plus, I feel pretty confident I might already know the things he is going to talk about. I'm sure my body will feel like collapsing into a pile of mush from the overwhelming stress I put myself through. But at least my day will have been productive with all my busyness, and the important thing is that everyone will be aware of how hard I worked and all I had accomplished. I will be the shining star at my own party. Maybe I'll have time for Jesus when the party is over, but if not, no worries. I'll do it tomorrow. Or maybe the next day . . . or the next.

I can only imagine the Martha we read about in the Bible, a friend of Jesus, may have felt this same way when Jesus and his seventy-two friends came to her house for a dinner party. Her chore list would certainly sound different than mine, considering she lived in biblical times, but the overwhelming obsessive desire to make sure everything was perfect was surely the same.

Instead of waxing the hardwoods, she may have had to sweep all the dirt floors. And, instead of cleaning the blinds, she may have had to hand wash the burlap cloths hanging over the window openings. But, despite which chores she was focused on, it is obvious she was focused on the chores—possibly fueled by an addiction to adrenaline and busyness or recognition—rather than quietly preparing to spend time with Jesus upon his arrival. Unfortunately, even after he arrived and she was in his presence, Martha still could not refrain from being busy and stressed. Her focus was in all the wrong places, which allowed stress to fill her day instead of peace, even with Jesus on the way to her house.

We shouldn't be too hard on poor Martha and can't really blame her for feeling that way. After all, I feel sure that she wanted her house to be clean and her food to be delicious, just as I would. I have worn myself plum frazzled before when preparing for a party at my house. So, in the same way, she probably just wanted her guests to be pleased and her hard work to be noticed, just as I would. She wanted her busyness to be a sign of her dedication and her success to symbolize her importance, just as I would. She wanted people to think she had the perfect home, the perfect family, and the perfect life. She wanted people to know how she had stressed over her preparations, so that they would appreciate her even more. She wanted to feel important. She wanted to know that she was doing a good thing—but what she didn't realize was that she was choosing the wrong "good thing." Jesus was the good thing. But she was too busy.

We live in a world where being an adrenaline junkie is considered a positive character trait. A world where we are expected to be all things to all people, juggling careers and families and daily pressure and crises, while keeping stress and anxiety at bay and maintaining the façade that we have it all together.

We are expected to push through our problems, pull ourselves up by our bootstraps, mask our emotions, and keep on trucking. We have been trained to believe we must keep going, and going, and going, like the Energizer bunny, without ever taking time to slow down, acknowledge our own needs, or worry about our stress level or our health.

Productivity becomes the indicator of our worth, and accomplishments drive our sense of purpose. We get trapped in the mindset of thinking that anxiety and depression are to be expected and accepted. And as a result of the demanding 24/7 culture we live in, we have come to believe that we have no choice but succumb to a life of chaos—even if it means living a life void of any peace or joy.

We have been brainwashed by the world that stress is normal and that we are to live in that normal, whether we like it or not. Worst of all, we convince ourselves that nothing can be done, but, in all honestly, nothing could be further from the truth.

Unfortunately, my made-up scenario of preparing for guests and Martha's story alike are prime examples of one day in the life of someone who allows stress to control their existence and who puts their focus on priorities that pale in comparison to what's really important. These stories serve to show us how even when we are doing good things, we can inadvertently allow the chaos and pulls of life to cause us to keep pushing Jesus further and further away, always thinking we'll make time for him "tomorrow" when we're not so busy, stressed, or pulled in so many directions. Tomorrow, we'll make him a priority and depend on him and his peace. The problem is, more often than not, tomorrow never comes. And that is when life starts going downhill and stress morphs into a poison that inflicts irreparable damage on every area of our lives.

According to the words of Jesus, a stressed-out life is not at all the way we are called to live. In fact, it is exactly the opposite. Jesus calls us to choose something better.

The Choice Is Yours

Mary and Martha were sisters, and Lazarus was their brother. They all lived together in the town of Bethany, just a few miles outside of Jerusalem. The three of them were close friends of Jesus, which is why he chose to stay at their home in the first place the week before his crucifixion. According to the book of Luke, Martha was the head of this household, and she was the first one to welcome Jesus into her home. Mary was probably the younger sister, and, just like in every family since the beginning of time, sibling rivalry obviously existed.

Let's take a look at this story in Luke 10:38–42:

> As Jesus and his disciples were on their way, he came
> to a village where a woman named Martha opened her
> home to him. She had a sister called Mary, who sat at
> the Lord's feet listening to what he said. But Martha was
> distracted by all the preparations that had to be made.
> She came to him and asked, "Lord, don't you care that
> my sister has left me to do the work by myself? Tell her to
> help me!"
>
> "Martha, Martha," the Lord answered, "you are wor-
> ried and upset about many things, but only one thing is
> needed. Mary has chosen what is better, and it will not
> be taken away from her." (NIV)

Although Scripture doesn't come out and say it directly, it is entirely possible (as is the case with most sisters) that Martha felt as if her little sister Mary had always been lazy, never helping around the house as much as she should, which resulted in her lack of patience at Mary's obvious negligence to help. Or perhaps Martha had already asked Mary several times to help her in the kitchen that day before she demanded that Jesus make Mary help.

This certainly happened quite often in my house when my children were younger! So, in consideration of the fact that Jesus was the most respected guest in the house that day, Martha chose him as the one who would have the authority to force her sister to help her. I find it bewildering that she did not *ask* if Jesus would mind telling Mary to help, but instead she *demanded* that he tell her to help. Oh, have mercy, what was Martha thinking?! Did she not realize whom she was talking to?

Had her pride over her accomplishments poisoned her thoughts, causing her to think she was more important than others? Had her frustration and resentment caused her to forget that Jesus stood for peace and love, not tension and demands? Had her habit of busyness pushed her to believe being busy was better than making time to be with Jesus? Had the many distractions of her life clouded her mind, making her lose sight of the fact Jesus was the Son of God, not merely a houseguest? Had her perspective on what was most important in life been skewed because of the pressure she was under? Had Martha become so stressed about that day, and possibly many days and months leading up to that day, she had forgotten the importance of relaxing and enjoying life? Of course, we have no way of knowing what was really in Martha's heart or mind, but her actions seem to imply the answer to each of these questions might be a resounding "yes."

On the other hand, Mary did have the right perspective. She was apparently a woman who allowed her heart to guide her actions—not busyness, stress, or worries about what other people thought. In this story in Luke, we see her sitting at the feet of Jesus, even though chaos and responsibilities were swarming all around her. Later, in John 12:3, we see her anointing the feet of Jesus with expensive perfume, wiping it with her hair. Mary wanted to learn from Jesus, depend on Jesus, and sit in his presence, saturating her heart with the peace she knew Jesus offered, even if other people didn't "get it."

Martha, on the other hand, had become so involved in her stress, her duties, and her own agenda that she didn't have time to learn from, depend on, or sit with Jesus. She lost her focus on what was important. As a result, she experienced stress instead of peace, because she was "worried and upset about many things."

The story about Martha and Mary ends after Jesus tells Martha she is wrong and Mary is right. We are given no indication of whether or not the response from Jesus had a lasting impact on Martha's spirit. However, we can make sure it has a lasting impact on us.

If you started out reading this book "worried and upset about many things," I pray your heart has been changed to be more like Mary's and less like Martha's. I pray you now have a heart that recognizes not only the seriousness of living under the weight of a stressed-out life, but also that Jesus is the answer to peace and serenity in this world characterized by chaos and stress.

Friends, my fervent prayer is that God has spoken loudly to your spirit and that through the pages of this journey we have taken together, your eyes have been opened to the consequences of a lifestyle plagued by toxic stress. I hope you have a new desire and inner passion to seek out God's peace every single day and expect to live with peace in your heart, even when life is chaotic and circumstances are hard.

I pray God has moved in your life in ways only he could do, and that you have come to recognize the importance of turning your stress over to him.

Yet, let's face it, despite how strong you may feel right now in your faith or how passionate you are about pursuing a less-stressed life from this point forward, the fact remains that life will continue on as normal. Those stressful circumstances you had yesterday will still be there tomorrow. With each passing day, stumbling blocks will, without a doubt, roll into our paths and threaten to pull the rug of peace we so confidently claimed to stand on right out from underneath us. Difficult circumstances will threaten our peace, stressful situations may fly in like a swarm of angry bees, and existing and new problems may cause our faith to be stretched. In our human frailty, it will be all too easy to default back into a habit of responding and reacting out of the flesh, allowing our emotions to cloud our thoughts, and our stress to become the stronghold over our lives rather than resting at the feet of Jesus in the midst of it all, as Mary did.

Although our peace can never be taken from us, we can relinquish it inadvertently when life gets difficult, circumstances seem hopeless, or the rush of adrenaline threatens to poison our hearts again. I say this not to discourage you but to warn you: Peace is not a destination. It is a process and takes an ongoing daily commitment, but the reward is worth the effort.

Let us take comfort in remembering that the Lord's mercies are renewed every day, and that each new wave of peace is only a prayer away.

Lamentations 3:22–24: "The faithful love of the LORD never ends! His mercies never cease. Great is his faithfulness; his mercies begin afresh each morning. I say to myself, 'The LORD is my inheritance; therefore, I will hope in him!'"

Keeping in Step

When we're stretched thin and about to snap, keeping our hearts in step with Jesus is the number one solution to living a less stressed life. We cannot do this thing called life on our own, and he never intended for us to in the first place.

If we long to have a feeling of peace in our hearts, even when our earthly lives are far from peaceful, we must never forget to make Jesus the most important part of each day. He doesn't expect us to stay in perfect step with him, because that is obviously not possible in our sinful nature. But he calls us to do our best to mirror his footsteps and walk in his ways. He does not expect us to walk without stumbling, but he does want us to always look to him for help when we fall.

In Ephesians 4:2–3 God offers a few tips for keeping our lives in step: "Be completely humble and gentle; be patient, bearing with one another in love. Make every effort to keep the unity of the Spirit through the bond of peace" (NIV). And in Galatians 5:22–23, we see a few more ways to walk in his steps: "But the Holy Spirit produces this kind of fruit in our lives: love, joy, peace, patience, kindness, goodness, faithfulness, gentleness, and self-control. There is no law against these things!"

These verses portray the inner fruits we need to harvest in our hearts if we desire for our outward actions to keep in step with what is important to Jesus. If our goal is to never return to a stressed-out, chaotic life, void of joy and peace and true happiness, then it's a good idea to pay close attention to God's suggestions. These fruits are the foundations for living the stress-less life, and once our hearts are in step with Jesus, the real journey to peace can begin.

Even though it may seem impossible to imagine, it is possible to trade in your stress for God's perfect peace. It may not happen overnight, but it will happen because although your circumstances may be the same, your heart will not be.

Just like anything worth having, an intimate relationship with our Holy Savior takes devotion and dedication. A life that is less stressed takes a daily commitment of tapping into the spiritual strength of God so we can get through life without allowing it to get to us. If we are hungry for the peace only God can provide, committing to change and doing whatever it takes to truly get to know the Prince of Peace will be a game changer.

As we focus on growing our relationship with him, we can still allow ourselves to enjoy the positive stress-relief outlets the world has to offer. Personally, I love a good massage, a relaxing pedicure, and a nap on the beach as the sounds of the surf soothe my soul. I love to play tennis and golf; exercise daily; watch a funny, mindless movie; and listen to soft music while enjoying scented candles. There is absolutely nothing wrong with enjoying things that make us feel rejuvenated and reenergized, and there is no need to feel guilty for enjoying life's simple pleasures. We just need to bear in mind that no matter how good those things feel in the moment, they will always only bring temporary peace, while real peace, the serenity that changes the course of our lives, will come from Jesus alone.

Isaiah 26:3 says, "You will keep in perfect peace all who trust in you, all whose thoughts are fixed on you!" This verse sums up the entire message of this book in one sentence because when our minds are focused and fixed on Jesus and our lives are centered around trusting him every day in every circumstance, we will have a level of tranquility in our hearts and our minds that we never thought possible.

Friends, your life is not going to change because you read a book about stress. Your life is going to change when you realize the absence of God and his peace in your life is intensifying the presence of stress in your heart.

Stress is an outward indication of an inner situation—a situation of a heart that needs Jesus. Only when we realize our need for him will we discover true peace in this less than peaceful world.

Life is complicated, but faith is not. As soon as you embrace the truth that Jesus is the only real source of peace, you will be able to begin embarking on a stress-less life. You will feel lighter, less stretched, and less stressed, even if your circumstances remain the same.

⤳ Reflection Questions

1. What "chores" might be keeping you too busy for Jesus? What shifts can you make to prioritize what's truly most important in life?

2. Have you ever felt too exhausted to spend time with Jesus? Explain a time when this happened, or admit if that describes your life right now. How might your life feel different if you made time to spend with him each day, despite the pull of your daily responsibilities?

3. Have you pushed Jesus to the back burner because daily responsibilities or stressors consumed all your time? Make a list of changes you can implement to ensure Jesus is put at the top of your daily to-do list. Pick two to three things from your list and intentionally commit to begin making them a habit in your life, starting today. Write them down and hang them up somewhere, so you'll be reminded to stick to your commitments each day!

4. Consider the steps mentioned regarding staying in step with Jesus: humility, gentleness, patience, love, unity with God, joy, kindness, goodness, faithfulness, self-control. In what ways might you be "out of step" with Jesus? Think of a few ways you could practice getting back into step and planting seeds for these fruits to begin blossoming in your life.

5. Of the steps you listed above, which ones should you make a priority in your life right now? How would focusing on improving in these areas help you achieve peace?

6. If you were to insert your name into the questions pondered about Martha earlier in this chapter, what would your answers be? Jot your honest answers down after each question, and ask God to help you overcome any heart issues that might be preventing you from resting at his feet.

- Has pride over your accomplishments poisoned your thoughts, causing you to think you are more important than others?

- Has frustration and resentment caused you to forget that Jesus stands for peace and love, not tension and demands?

- Has your habit of busyness caused you to believe that being busy is better than spending downtime with Jesus and the people you love?

- Have the many distractions of your life clouded your mind, making you lose sight of the fact that Jesus is the Son of God? Are you taking him for granted?

- Has your perspective on what is most important in life been skewed because of the pressures you are under?

- Have you become so stressed, because of your circumstances and overwhelming emotions that you have forgotten the importance of relaxing and enjoying life, trusting that Jesus has everything under control?

If your answer is "yes" to any or all of these questions, then know you need to make a commitment to set aside some quiet time in the next twenty-four hours for praying to God, seeking his face, asking for his guidance and perspective on the situations in your life, and searching for wisdom and clarity about the changes that you might need to make within yourself. Consider planning a miniretreat, where you and God are the only attendees.

7. Do you now believe with your whole heart Jesus is the only true solution for stress? Write a prayer of praise and thankfulness for the peace Jesus offers, including your promise to always seek his face and keep your thoughts fixed on him so that when stress rises in your life, your peace will rise higher.

Stress-Busting Scriptures

I wait quietly before God,
for my victory comes from him.
He alone is my rock and my salvation,
my fortress where I will never be shaken.

Psalm 62:1–2

❧

The LORD says, "I will rescue those who love me.
I will protect those who trust in my name.
When they call on me, I will answer;
I will be with them in trouble.
I will rescue and honor them.
I will reward them with a long life
and give them my salvation."

Psalm 91:14–16

❧

But for you who fear my name,
the Sun of Righteousness will rise with healing in his wings.
And you will go free,
leaping with joy like calves let out to pasture.

Malachi 4:2

❧

The name of the LORD is a strong fortress;
the godly run to him and are safe.

Proverbs 18:10

❧

You are worried and upset about many things,
but only one thing is needed.

Luke 10:41b–42a NIV

❧

Notes

[1] American Psychological Association, "Stress in America 2020: Stress in the Time of COVID-19, Volume One," May 2020, https://www.apa.org/news/press/releases/stress/2020/report.

[2] "Adult Obesity Rates," State of Childhood Obesity, September 2020, https://stateofchildhoodobesity.org/adult-obesity/.

[3] "A Discussion of Stress: The Stress Epidemic," The StressFree Network, accessed October 21, 2011, http://www.stressfree.com/stress.html.

[4] American Psychological Association, "Stress in America 2020: A National Mental Health Crisis," October 2020, https://www.apa.org/news/press/releases/stress/2020/report-october.

[5] American Psychological Association, "Stress in America 2020: A National Mental Health Crisis."

[6] Kara Perez, "How to Build Your Willpower and Self-Control," Due.com, February 19, 2017, https://due.com/blog/build-will-power/.

[7] R. A. Clay, "Stressed in America," *Monitor on Psychology* 42, no. 1 (Jan. 2011): 60, http://www.apa.org/monitor/2011/01/stressed-america.aspx.

[8] Daniel K. Hall-Flavin, "Can Chronic Stress Cause Depression?" Mayo Clinic, March 24, 2020, http://www.mayoclinic.com/health/stress/AN01286.

[9] "Stress Symptoms: Effects on Your Body and Behavior," Mayo Clinic, April 04, 2019, http://www.mayoclinic.org/healthy-lifestyle/stress-management/in-depth/stress-symptoms/art-20050987.

[10] Christine Lehmann, "Pandemic Drives Couples to Divorce or to Seek Help," WebMD, November 7, 2020, https://www.webmd.com/lung/news/20201207/pandemic-drives-couples-to-divorce-or-to_seek-help.

[11] Jolynn Tumolo, "COVID-19 Stress Taking Toll on Parent-Child Relationships," Psychiatry and Behavioral Health Learning Network, April

13, 2020, https://www.psychcongress.com/article/covid-19-stress-taking-toll -parent-child-relationships.

[12] "Workplace Stress: A Silent Killer of Employee Health and Productivity, *Corporate Wellness Magazine*, accessed April 13, 2021, https://www .corporatewellnessmagazine.com/article/workplace-stress-silent-killer -employee-health-productivity.

[13] Max Lucado, *In the Eye of the Storm* (Dallas: Word Publishing, 1991), 54.

[14] Krista Mahr, "How Stress Harms the Heart," *Time,* October 9, 2007, http://www.time.com/time/health/article/0,8599,1669766,00.html.

[15] American Psychological Association, "Stress in America 2020: A National Mental Health Crisis."